STINKERS:

America's Worst Self-Published Books

Learn what not to do

(Volume I)

Michael N. Marcus

SILVER SANDS BOOKS
www.SilverSandsBooks.com

195 Magnolia Road
Milford CT 06461
books@ablecomm.com
203-878-8383

ISBN-13: 978-0-9830572-5-3
Library of Congress Control Number: 2011914029
Printed in the USA
Version 1.71 (CS-9 1002011)

Please use the physical or email addresses on the previous page for corrections, questions and comments.

Portions of this book were previously published in other Silver Sands books
or online.

Editor: Mark Shields
Cover photo from DRB Images

Notes: ①This book's purpose is to educate, inform, instruct and entertain. ②While this book should be helpful, no book can tell you everything that you might want to know or need to know about the
topics it tries to cover. ③Some errors may not have been detected
and corrected. ⑤Neither the author nor the publisher will be held li-
able or responsible for any actual or perceived loss or damage to any
person or entity, caused or alleged to have been caused, directly or
indirectly, by anything in this book. If you won't accept these terms,
please stop reading.

More about the author: www.MichaelMarc.us
Help & info for self-publishers: www.BookFur.com
Early book evaluation: www.RentABookReviewer.com

Create Better Books with the
Silver Sands Publishing Series
www.silversandsbooks.com/booksaboutpublishing.html

Also by Michael N. Marcus

Books:

- Independent Self-Publishing: The Complete Guide (2011)
- Self-Publish Your Book Without Losing Your Shirt (2011)
- A Self-Published Book Doesn't Have to be Ugly (2011)
- Get the Most out of a Self-Publishing Company (2011)
- The 100 Worst Self-Publishing Misteaks (co-author, 2011)
- 555 Ways to Self-Publish Better Books (2011)
- 399 Valuable Self-Publishing Tips for a Penny Apiece (2011)
- Internet Hell (2011)
- Easy E-books (2011)
- Become a <u>Real</u> Self-Publisher (2010)
- Stupid, Sloppy, Sleazy (2010)
- Stories I'd Tell My Children (2010)
- What I Most Wanted to Get Out of School Was Me (2010)
- Phone Systems & Phones for Small Business & Home (2009)
- The AbleComm Guide to Phone Systems (2009)
- Telecom Reference E-book (2009)
- I Only Flunk My Brightest Students (2008)
- What Phone System Should I Buy? (1996)
- CB Bible (co-author, 1976)

Blogs:

- **Book Making** is where Michael discusses writing, editing and publishing—and other things that interest him or bother him. www.BookMakingBlog.blogspot.com
- **My Final Quarter-Century Above Ground** deals with dying and death—with appropriate irreverence. www.BloggingAboutDeath.blogspot.com
- **911 Wackos.** Some folks call 911 for strange reasons. Sometimes they get into trouble after the call. Sometimes the 911 operators get into trouble. www.911Wackos.blogspot.com
- **For The First Time (or the last time)** talks about changes in society and technology: first toilet paper, last country to get TV, etc. www.4TheFirstTime.blogspot.com
- **Oh How Stupid** provides an occasional look at some of the stupidest things done by human beings. www.OhHowStupid.blogspot.com
- **Letters to April Wong** is a collection of ridiculous and scam emails sent to a person who does not exist. www.LettersToAprilWong.blogspot.com
- **Dial Zero** discusses what's silly, stupid or surprising in telecom. www.DialZero.blogspot.com

There may be more by the time you read this.

"From the moment I picked your book up until I laid it down I was convulsed with laughter. Someday I intend reading it."
Groucho Marx
(1890-1977)

"This is not a novel to be tossed aside lightly. It should be thrown with great force."
Dorothy Parker
(1893–1967)

"It is far better to be silent than merely to increase the quantity of bad books."
Voltaire
(1694-1778)

"A good novel tells us the truth about its hero; but a bad novel tells us the truth about its author."
Gilbert K. Chesterton
(1874-1936)

"We publish a huge number of really bad books."
Bob Young, founder of Lulu.com

If Bob knows they're really bad books, he shouldn't publish them. Bob also misspelled "misspell" and confused "less" and "fewer." A publisher should know better.

"Errors in your writing cause readers to question your credibility."
Brent Sampson, founder of Outskirts Press

In one of Brent's books, he wrote the wrong name of the publisher of *Roget's Thesaurus* and made many other errors. A publisher should do better.

Introduction

The book publishing business is changing significantly and rapidly, and the changes provide both limitations and opportunities for authors.

BAD NEWS:

1. Sales of books by bookstores are decreasing and bookstores are closing.
2. Surviving bookstores face growing competition from other types of businesses and from e-books.
3. It has become much harder for new writers to get published by traditional publishers.
4. Traditional publishers have fired employees and cut back on the number of books selected, author advances and promotional budgets.
5. Mergers and acquisitions have reduced the number of major publishing houses.
6. Most publishers judge books based on potential profitability rather than on literary merit.
7. Most terrestrial bookstores won't stock self-published books.
8. Some book review media reject self-published books.
9. Some authors' associations ban self-publishing authors from membership.

GOOD NEWS:

1. Online booksellers Amazon.com, BarnesAndNoble.com and dozens of others worldwide make a huge selection of books—including self-published books—available quickly to anyone, anywhere.
2. In 2008, for the first time, sales of print on demand ("POD") books (which include most self-published books) exceeded sales of traditionally printed books. The number of POD titles has been growing by triple digits in recent years.
3. Independent publishers are following the path of "indie" musicians and filmmakers by cutting out the middlemen between the creators and the audience.
4. Technology has made it much simpler and less expensive for any writer to have a book published, either on paper or electronically, without approval by the gatekeepers of traditional publishing.
5. There are many ways to get inexpensive or free publicity.
6. Many businesses are eager to sell publishing and distribution services to authors. They are able to produce excellent books—and terrible books.
7. More and more online venues review self-published books, and new organizations and online communities support self-publishing authors.

Although it has become relatively easy to self-publish, it's also easy to make serious mistakes in writing, design and marketing that can seriously limit the acceptability and sales of a self-published book.

While there is great satisfaction in seeing your name on the cover of a book, I hope that you will write what other people will want to read, and that they'll like what you write.

I believe in absolute freedom of the press. I don't believe in prior censorship or the licensing of writers or publishers. Unfortunately, the ease of publication means that a lot of junk gets published.

It's sad—and funny—that some of the worst self-published books I've found, and the majority of the books in *this* book, are books that try to provide advice to other authors.

This book will help you avoid the worst mistakes of others, so you can publish a book that you can be justifiably proud of, and perhaps enlighten, entertain and inform others—and maybe you'll even make some money.

Michael

What makes a book a stinker?

1. Most stinkers are ugly.
2. Most stinkers are poorly written.
3. Most stinkers violate the rules and customs of book design.
4. Many stinkers are inaccurate.
5. Some stinkers make promises they do not—or cannot—deliver.
6. Some stinkers are padded—including unnecessary information, information that is readily available elsewhere for free, or too much empty space.
7. Some stinkers are really advertisements—even bad advertisements—masquerading as books.
8. Some stinkers are absurdly overpriced.
9. Some stinker authors either got help from the wrong people or got no help at all.
10. Some stinker authors are extremely careless—or just don't care about producing good books.
11. Some stinker authors don't accept the advice they give to others.
12. Some stinker authors know less than they think they know.

Contents

What's a "self-published" book?

In this book, I generally mean a book produced by a "self-publishing company" (the kind of company that used to be called a "vanity press," "vanity publisher," "subsidy publisher" or even "author mill"). Because most of these companies will publish any book that is not obscene or libelous, and they don't insist on editing, they publish a lot of terrible books. I sometimes use the term to indicate a book published by a company owned by the book's author or the author's family.

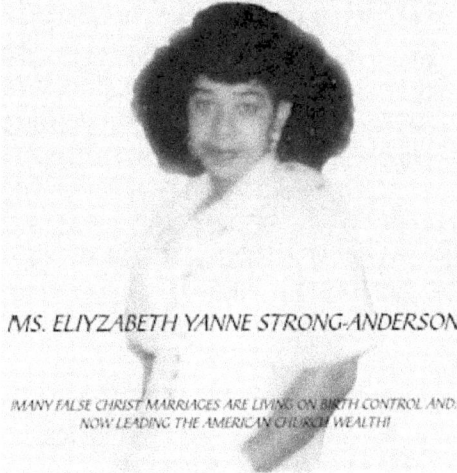

BIRTH CONTROL IS SINFUL IN THE
CHRISTIAN MARRIAGES and also
ROBBING GOD OF PRIESTHOOD
CHILDREN!!

MS. ELIYZABETH YANNE STRONG-ANDERSON

MANY FALSE CHRIST MARRIAGES ARE LIVING ON BIRTH CONTROL AND
NOW LEADING THE AMERICAN CHURCH WEALTH!

Birth Control is Sinful in the Christian Marriages and also Robbing God of Priesthood Children!
Eliyzabeth Yanne Strong-Anderson
AuthorHouse, 2008, 648 pages, $150

#1 **This is probably the worst book ever published! It has 648 huge pages, $150 cover price and an Amazon sales rank below 10,000,000. No lowercase letters are used in the book. It's ugly, has bad grammar, bad spelling and atrocious typography. Also, the title is stupid and the theme is absurd.**

Quoted, without editing:

ARE YOU BARREN AND DISGUSTED?? OR BIRTH CONTROLING AND BUSTED?? THESE QUESTIONS IS >ONE OF THE MOST IMPORTANT CHAPTERS IN THIS BOOK: > REVEALING > THE SINS OF THE CHURCHES: REVEALING: HOW *THE SINS BIRTH CONTROL IN OUR CHRISTIAN MARRIAGES AND IN THE WORLD MARRIAGES EVEN IN SINFUL SEXUAL RELATIONSHIPS: HAS CALLED WORLD SIN IN ADULTERY AND FORNICATING RELATIONSHIP AND FALSE CHRIST LEADERSHIP. >THE PIT OF SPIRITUAL WHOREDOM BECAME OPEN AND THE CAUSE OF ORGANIZED CRIME IN OUR GOVERNMENT AND WORLD LEADERSHIP

THE YEAR OF 1994. THE MILITARY HELP DESTROY MY **MARRIAGE OF 17 YEARS. FALSE CHRIST LEADERSHIPS BEGAN** TO FORM ON TELEVISION.

BECAUSE OF SPIRITUAL SEDUCING SINS. AND SPIRITUAL DARKNESS IN OUR CHURCHE LEADERSHIP.

BELIEVE IT OR NOT: BIRTH CONTROL IS ONE OF THE MAJOR REASON: WHY HUMANS HAVE FALLEN FAILED COMES COMMANDMENTS: AND NOW THEY HAVE BECOME: WARFUL AGAIN: HEARTLESS AND SINFULLY PERSECUTING CHRISTIANS AND HOLY PEOPLE IN MANY COUTRIES. ** SINFULLY STARTING PERSECUTIONS AND RACISM: THROUGH EMPLOYMENT DISCRIMINATIONS. **RESULTING IN GREED AND EVIL: EVEN WORLD WHOREDOM: CAUSING > HOMOSEXUAL AND GAY SINS: USING THE MEDIA OF TELEVISION, THE INTERNET WIDE WORLD WEBSITES AND RADIO SATANIC WORSHIP.

MY FIRST CHRISTIAN BOOK: ASK THE QUESTIONS:

ARE YOU BARREN AND DISGUSTED?? OR> . BIRTHCONTROLING AND BUSTED?? >REMINDING THE

WORLD: > ONE IS A SIN AND THE OTHER IS A CURSE OR PERSECUTION!!

JESUS SAID: YOU CANNOT SERVE TWO MASTERS: BECAUSE > YOU WILL LEARN TO HATE ONE! > AND LOVE THE OTHER!! **

WOMEN AND CHRISTIAN MARRAIGES ON BIRTH CONTROL HAVE LEARN TO HATE HAVING CHILDREN: AND LOVE LIVING WITHOUT THEM. *CAUSING WORK DISCRIMINATIONS AGAINST WOMEN WHO DO HAVE SMALL CHILDREN. AND CAUSING DISCRIMINATIONS: AGAINST OUR CHILDRENS FUTURE BY STARTING WARS AND BY WRITING LAWS AGAINST SCHOOL PROSPERITY.

MY AUTHOR NAME IS: MS. ELIYZABETH YANNE STRONG-ANDERSON: I AM A HOLYSPIRIT ANOINTED CHOSEN DISCIPLE OF GOD AND CHRIST JESUS. NAMED TO BE A ANOINTED APOSTLE TEACHER BY THE VOICE OF GOD: TO HELP CALLED THE TRUE CHRISTIAN CHURCH INTO TRUE ETERNAL LIFE SALVATION IN JOHN 3:16. THIS BOOK IS DIRECTED BY GODS HOLYSPIRIT VOICE: ALSO BASE ON THE HOLY COMMANDMENTS: EXODUS 20:13 THOU SHALT NOT KILL, GENESIS 1:26-31 GO INCREASE, MULTIPLY AND TAKE DOMINIONSHIP OVER ALL THINGS. AND 1TIMOTHY 2;15 *THE WOMEN WILL BE SAVED IN CHILD BEARING YEARS: IF SHE CONTINUES: WITH FAITH, CHARITY AND HOLINESS. *ALSO REVELATIONS 2 & 3:*GOD IS ASKING THE CHURCHES TO REPENT OF ALL THEIR> SINS: AND TO RESTORE THE TRUE CHURCH BACK INTO GOD EVER LASTING COMMANDMENTS. * GOD HAS CALLED AND CHOSEN: ELIYZABETH TO HELP SAVED THE WORLD AND CHURCH FROM THE FALSE CHRIST TEACHINGS. *THROUGH THIS BOOK HOLYSPIRIT PRAYERS: AND HOLYSPIRIT TEACHINGS: YOU WILL AND CAN FIND TRUE SALVATION IN GOD AND CHRIST JESUS: JOHN 3:3-16 THIS HOLYSPIRIT BOOK OF REPENTANCE AND REMEMBER OF THE WORDS AND COMMANDMENTS OF GOD: WILL HELP YOU BECOME A TRUE: BORN AGAIN CHRISTIAN: JOHN 3:3-16

REMEMBER: JESUS SAID: YOU MUST BE BORN AGAIN: OF THE WATER AND OF THE SPIRIT . GOD HAS DIRECTED*ELIYZABETH HOLYSPIRIT WRITINGS IN THIS BOOK TO HELP ALL>UNDERSTAND GODS SALVATION CALLS!! GOD HAS DIRECTED THIS BOOK TO HELP ALL WHO SEEK TO BE OBEDIENT TO GODS HOLY COMMANDMENTS: EVEN OVERCOME ALL FALSE CHRIST TEACHINGS: THROUGH REPENTENCE & RESTORATION: GIVING GODS TITHES BACK INTO THE HOLYSPIRIT LEADERSHIP: STARTING WITH: THIS BOOK OF HOLYSPIRIT SERVANT: MS. ELIYZABETH YANNE STRONG-ANDERSON: WHEN YOU GIVE TO MY HOLYSPIRIT DISCIPLESHIP: YOU CAN BE SURE YOUR ETERNAL LIFE AND NAME WILL BE WRITTEN IN THE LAMBS BOOK OF LIFE. **SUPPORT GODS HOLYSPIRIT GOALS: THROUGH THIS HOLYSPIRIT BOOK WITH YOUR CHRISTIAN CHARITY

This book has attracted a huge number of reviews on Amazon.com, mostly from people who have never read the book, but just want to be part of the fun. Here are some (unedited) examples:

(1) Well,I'm very grateful I came across this book. I was going to do the 'sensible' thing and plan my family according to my income,health and emotional issues,but now I realise I was wrong & sinful for wanting to have a 'manageable' number of kids.Unfortunately my spouse likes to do the wild thing a LOT and I now have 20 of God's little miracles to feed.Thankfully,I've been able to take a rest from my marital obligations lately as he's either left me or I've lost him under the pile of nappies.A shame,really,as permanently being in maternity clothes makes dressing choices in the morning SO much easier.Oh,well,the nappies come in handy for my untreated obstetric fistula.

We're now living under a bridge,& I can no longer afford my anti-pychotic medication but God will provide.Especially as we're planning on eating little Arthur on Tuesday.If I sell Becky to the knackers we'll have food til Thursday.Now,excuse me,I must go.Eustace is near the drain hole poking something nasty with a stick and the blue goblins are telling me to drown Egibald.Which is insane.Eugenia is the one that has to go.Anyway,this book is a godsend for those days I feel inexplicably depressed & can't connect to my children.Probably just need to pray more.Eustace! I told you! Put that stick down now! You don't know where that dead body has been!!

My one criticism is that the font is small and hard to read by candlelight. Other than that,it's a brilliant book.Thick enough to kill the cockroaches . . . .

(2) Despite being written entirely in BLOCK CAPITALS, this self-published work conveys its message elegantly. In fact, you don't even need to read it to understand the main argument being put forward.

True, by avoiding this book you will miss out on the precise location of the heretical surfboard worshipped by the British royal family and the sinister significance of Abe Lincoln's unholy quadrille. You will also miss out on the explanation of why the Hairy-Eared Dwarf Lemur is really God's own tree-dwelling angel-on-earth and on the coded instructions showing how to grow a prize-winning mushroom, which the author cunningly gleaned from a close textural analysis of St. Paul's third birthday card to the Corinthians.

That aside, my big problem with this book is that the 'birth control is sinful' message is difficult for most regular-looking people to put into practice. I wonder if this lack of guidance is down to the author's own sexual inexperience brought about by her scary fanaticism and a face that would scare a dog out of a butcher's shop.

(3) That's right kids. Don't be doing the sex thing. But if you are be doing the sex thing, don't be taking no pills or putting no rubber things on your ding dong to prevent god's babies.

After all, we need more crazy people to write more nonsense like this.

(4) I FINALLY UNDERSTAND THAT SEX IS NAUGHTY! AND MY GRAMMAR TEACHER DOESN'T REALLY MATTER BECAUSE I CAN MAKE A BOOK BY USING TYPO'S. THE BOOK REALLY MADE ME BELIEVE THAT SEX WASN'T MADE FOR PLEASURE BUT FOR BABIES. THEN GOD MUST HAVE REALLY FUDGED UP WHEN SHE MADE THE CLITORIS WHICH IS AN ORGAN COMPLETLY MADE FOR ONE THING...PLEASURE? WHICH SEX IS NOT ABOUT AT ALL BUT BABIES. ONLY SMELLY BABIES WHO WILL SERVE GOD IF I TEACH HIM ABOUT GOD....THIS BOOK HAS TAUGHT ME THAT I WILL MAKE SURE MY CHILDREN ARE RAISED THE RIGHT WAY TO HATE THEIR BODIES AND EVENTUALLY BECOME SO SEXUALLY REPRESSED THEY RIGHT A BOOK THAT NO PUBLISHING COMPANY WILL PUBLISH SO YOU SELL IT FOR 150 DOLLARS RETAIL.

AFTER READING THIS LIFE-CHANGING BOOK, I WANTED TO PAY HOMAGE TO THE BLOCK CAP. I WILL DO SO, HOWEVER, WITHOUT IT.

(5) The only thing that bothers me about the author's choice of capital letters is the fact that "block cap" sounds like a form of birth control. While I felt the author waffled

on the issue of weather or not using said methods were allowable in the Christian faith, the one thing she makes clear is that this book is worth all 138,000 pennies. If you note, the book is on sale (for a steal) from $150; I don't know why you wouldn't act now!

The thing that speaks to me is the author's choice of blue background with MS Paint style picture editing - simply genius! When reading this book in church or on a subway, everyone around you will know how serious you are by the cover alone (refer to my all capital letters point before). If anyone would like to contact me with questions before buying this book (like how much it will change your life forever, does Eliyzabeth Yanne Strong-Anderson the author answer your letters of admiration, or if you would be better off just not using a cockbag) please email.

(6) I HAD A SIT DOWN CONVERSATION WITH THE MAGIC MAN IN THE SKY WHO TELLS US IF WE HAVE SEX FOR FUN, WE'LL ALL DIE AND BE BURNED IN A LAKE OF BOILING LAVA FOR EVER AND EVER AND EVER AND WE'LL BE IN UNBEARABLE AGONY FOREVER, TORTURED BEYOND BELIEF. But he loves us!

So talk to the Flying Spaghetti Monster instead! He'll let you have sex for fun. So will the Invisible Pink Unicorn.

(7) Am I astounded by the psychotic sentence structure and "logic" of this book? Not at all. Deranged ideas, such as cranking out babies to increase the number of people who can be converted to your religious beliefs, deserve deranged presentation. Ms. Strong-Anderson is far more honest in her presentation than some others who oppose birth control on similar grounds.

ARE THE BLOCK CAPITALS OFF-PUTTING OR OVERLY DISTRACTING??? no, i don't find them so.

17

What? about the odd, and dis-jointed use of: punctuation?!? No, again, crazy is as crazy does.

The utter religious lunacy? Folks, I live in Topeka with a bunch of Phelpses. I see crazier and more hateful stuff than this on the street corners every day.

Here's the part I find truly offensive: that someone would have the unmitigated hubris required to think that this mound of verbiage deserves a price tag of one-hundred and thirty eight dollars. The only thing that would make me angrier than that is if there is some fool somewhere who actually gave this person money.

(8) I honestly don't know if this is a joke or not... Someone help me out here? Is this a gag, or what?

(9)There have been many incisive commentaries written here. But, curiously, they all omit the sine qua non of Ms. Strong-Anderson's talents as a writer: her mastery of both definite and indefinite articles. In the title itself, we, the readers, are told that Birth Control is Sinful in *the* Christian Marriages (emphasis mine). Not "in Christian Marriages", "in many Christian Marriages", or even "in most Christian Marriages". No, none of that for Strong-Anderson, who is clear that it is happening in THE Christian Marriages. We are naturally led to ask: yes, but WHICH?

That seemingly wee question leads the reader on a journey through prophylaxis, fertilization, betrothal, implantation (or lack thereof), larceny, theology, and much else besides. Including subtle omissions -- and commissions -- of English articles of various sorts. If you've ever wondered, even in your quietest moments, exactly in which Christian Marriages birth control is robbing God of priesthood children, this book was written with you in mind.

I bought your reasonably priced book, and it has been a gift from God. My children were fornicating unsuccessfully for years, but once they read this piece of magic they stopped instantly. They didn't even need to open it - the cover alone scared them back to the straight and narrow. Now the priesthood has two new children to fornicate with. That is what she meant, right?

I love you MS. ELIYZABETH YANNE STRONG and I DESIRE MUCH to make PRIESTHOOD CHILDREN with you. Christian power forever!

(10) I love this book. It has so many uses.

In the summer I can use it to hold the door open and in the winter to hold it closed. It's is weighty enough that I can use it to press my trousers, when placed in the window next to my front door, it scares off the door-to-door salesmen, thanks to the cheery faced Medusa on the cover.

If I'm hot I can fan myself and if cold, I can burn it. At the bargain price of $135 I can resell it and buy something I might want to read.

The inside pages can be removed to make into a paper mache mask, and the cover is good for crushing spiders.

As for the book's message? If I looked like the woman on the cover, I would never have to worry about birth control ever again.

Sarah Palin personally recommended this book to me. She gave it five stars. One for each kid.

(11) There are times in your life when you encounter the equivalent of a train wreck. You find something that is so excruciatingly awful that it transcends that awfulness and becomes a source of amusement and, dare I say, enter-

tainment. Seeing 'Plan Nine From Outer Space," or its modern counterpart, "Battlefield Earth," has this effect. At first you are shocked at the awfulness of the thing. Then you question it, is this a put-on, some sort of gag? Finally you realize that it really is just as supremely horrible as you had first suspected, but knowing this, you settle in for the long haul, reveling in the sheer masochistic joy that only comes from exposure to the sublimely asinine. Such is the case with this rare tome. Here is a woman who is clearly several bananas short of a fruit cocktail, a woman with a world-view that has only a passing acquaintance with reality, a woman who feels with absolute certainty that she is the designated mouthpiece of an almighty deity. She has taken one small part of her twisted world-view and took the time to write a book on the subject. She sums up the book entirely in its title, and yet feels the necessity to devote hours and perhaps days to pointless reiteration and abstraction of these concepts. Having completed this herculean task, she takes this text file, sans correction, and has the audacity to market it for one hundred thirty five freaking dollars! One can only marvel at the sheer egotism of this woman, to not only be God's appointed mouthpiece, but also to expect to profit so outrageously from God's given word. This is to the printed word what John Daker is to song. It is every bit as much a lunatic rant as the works of the late Francis E. Dec, but not nearly as entertaining, and with a much heftier price tag. It is also, in its way, terribly cliched, since Francis E. Dec and many others have already paved the way with their pioneer works of caps-locked, arbitrarily-punctuated, randomly portmanteaued babblings. This is just a more current example, and not nearly as much fun.

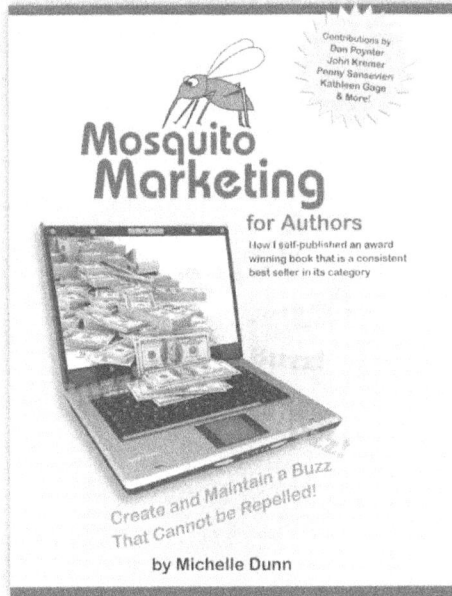

Mosquito Marketing for Authors
Michelle Dunn
CreateSpace, 2010, 174 pages, $12.95

#2

This book is the second-worst, and third-rate. It demonstrates what happens when a marketing expert who's a sloppy writer hires a designer who doesn't know how to design books and an editor who doesn't notice mistakes.

Mosquito Marketing for Authors

Never Dunn Publishing LLC • Plymouth, New Hampshire

By Michelle Dunn
©2010 Michelle Dunn

Published by:

Never Dunn Publishing LLC
PO Box 40
Plymouth NH 03264

www.michelledunn.com
www.credit-and-collections.com

Cover design, book layout, and production by
WoW! Graphic Designs www.wowgraphicdesigns.com • 800-962-4254

Author photos by Timothy Cameron, Achber Studio, Laconia, NH

Editing by provided by Arlene Stoppe

Library of Congress control Number: TX 6-205-251

This book is designed to provide accurate and authoritative information in regard to the subject matter covered. It is sold with the understanding that the author is not engaged in rendering legal advice or services. If legal advice is required, please see your attorney.

Printed in the United States of America.

Never Dunn
N
Publishing

← The title page contains material that belongs on the copyright page. It also has a silly editing error in the line about the editor: *"Editing by provided by Arlene Stoppe."*

The page has the name of Michelle's publishing company THREE TIMES. Once is enough. However, the book's ISBN (International Standard Book Number) is not provided even once on this page—or anywhere in the front matter.

The page shows what should be a Library of Congress Control Number (LCCN). Michelle strangely puts "control" in lowercase, and the number she shows is *not* an LCCN and I have *no* idea what it is.

The bottom of the page has a disclaimer warning readers not to use the book for legal advice. This is just one of *three disclaimers* which Michelle provides in the *first five pages*. She repeatedly warns the reader to consult an attorney. One disclaimer is enough. One disclaimer is enough.

The second disclaimer says that the author is not giving "professional advice." Sadly, the book contains a lot of UNprofessional advice. Oddly enough, that disclaimer, starts in the third person, switches to first person, and then goes back to third person.

©2010 Michelle Dunn

© COPYRIGHT 2009, MICHELLE A. DUNN

Which year do you prefer?

The first page—which is the wrong place to put it—indicates a copyright date of 2010, with the name "Michelle Dunn." However, if you don't like 2010, just flip the page. You will then see a copyright date of 2009, and here Michelle's name appears with the middle initial "A" and a comma before her name. Consistency is not Michelle's strong suit.

Reading this book was a very frustrating experience.

Michelle Dunn knows her subject well. Unfortunately, she is a careless (or maybe uncaring) author who chose an unqualified editor and designer, and together they produced a very bad book.

This book has 174 pages, but it has *more errors than pages*. It is so badly written, edited and designed that it can hurt the people it is intended to help. Its audience is new authors, and a new author who uses this book as an example for publishing a book will produce yet another bad book. We don't need more of them.

While this book is not specifically about producing a book, it's dangerous because newbies who read it and are impressed by its reviews and Michelle's apparent success may assume that it is a proper example of publishing.

Sadly, the author thinks that the book is fine. In an online discussion, Michelle wrote, "My proof came back perfect—woohoo!" Only someone who knows nothing about books or can't read or has extremely bad vision would think a proof of this book is perfect.

The book has 12 five-star reviews on Amazon.com. One is highly suspicious and may have been written by Michelle. Another five-star review was written by someone who wrote part of the book and may benefit from its success. Most of the reviewers were blind to the book's abundant errors. The one expert reviewer who noticed what is wrong with the book gave it the lowest rating possible.

Normally, in any effort—especially one from a "marketer extraordinaire"—people know to "put your best foot forward."

With a book, the best foot should be the front cover. Michelle's cover is dreadful, and the book gets worse as it progresses.

Michelle realized that the book needs two subtitles to explain what it's about. The second subtitle on the cover says that the book should enable readers to "Create and Maintain a Buzz That Cannot be Repelled."

Sorry, Michelle, a title should "work" without even *one* subtitle. A subtitle should AMPLIFY a title and provide additional searchable keywords. A title has to make sense without its subtitle—and Michelle's does not.

Imagine this conversation:
Sam: "Hi, Michelle. What's new?"
Michelle: "I just published a book."
Sam: "What's it called?"
Michelle: "Mosquito Marketing for Authors."
Sam: "What's it about?"

Sam should not have to ask that question. If someone can't discern the subject from a book's title, it's a bad title. (Note: this does not apply to novels or poetry and I hereby grant dispensation to the cover of the book you are now reading.)

The main illustration on the front cover is based on a stock photo which cost Michelle a few bucks. The photo could be part of a logo for a company that does PC repair or website design. It could be on a book about selling on eBay or Craigslist. But there is nothing about the illustration that is specifically tied to marketing books for authors.

The text on the front cover has problems with punctuation and the book is shown to be written "by Michelle Dunn." Sorry, Michelle, but the word "by" is seldom used with an author's name after third grade.

The sins on the back cover include:
- Amateur typography (straight quote marks instead of curly "typographer's marks"
- Bad punctuation

- Inconsistent uppercasing
- Bad writing
- A factual error
- Improper author's photo
- Strangely, Michelle decided to print an incomplete and unnecessary ISBN and an "EAN-13" below the logo on the bottom of the back cover. The full ISBN is printed above the barcode. "EAN" was originally "European Article Number," but is now used to mean "International Article Number"—and there is *no* need to have it on the book.

E ditor Arlene Stoppe's main business seems to be real estate. She may be Michelle's landlady or best buddy, but I could not find anything online—and certainly not in this book—that qualifies Arlene to be an editor.

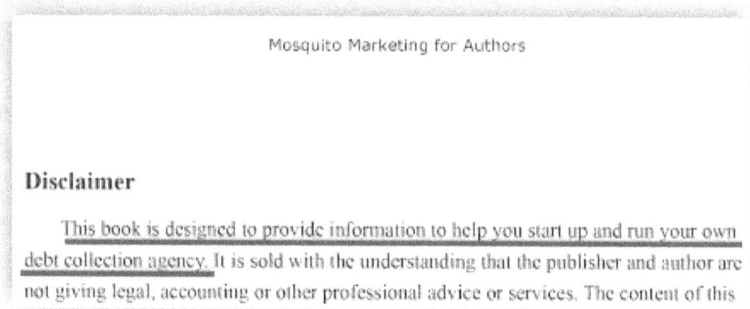

Mosquito Marketing for Authors

Disclaimer

This book is designed to provide information to help you start up and run your own debt collection agency. It is sold with the understanding that the publisher and author are not giving legal, accounting or other professional advice or services. The content of this

(above) Neither Arlene nor Michelle noticed that the second page tells us that "This book is designed to provide information to help you start up and run your own DEBT COLLECTION AGENCY." That's right. Michelle stupidly copied material from a previous book about an *entirely different subject* and pasted it, unread and unedited, into the mosquito book.

I don't want to write an entire book about Michelle Dunn's book, so I'll just list a few more of her many infractions.

- Michelle's biography appears in the book at least TWELVE times. Once is enough.
- The book contains more than eight pages written by other authors—which you can read at no cost online.
- Missing, misplaced, improper and doubled punctuation marks of all types
- Improper, misplaced and misspelled words
- The book recommends a website that is published in Japanese and has links to other Japanese websites. Maybe Michelle reads Japanese. I wonder how many of her readers do.
- The Table of Contents ("TOC") shows a different version of the second subtitle.
- The TOC includes items on pages *before* the TOC.
- The TOC has errors.
- The TOC is much too long and much too detailed, but there is *no index*—bad for a how-to book.
- Frequent unnecessary and inconsistent uppercasing
- Inconsistent spelling
- Inconsistent use of the ampersand and the word "and"
- Lack of italics on most (but not all) names of publications
- Use of an apostrophe plus "s" to form many plurals
- Nonsensical sequences of words, such as "Since libraries are good pay but only order one book each . . . ."
- Just plain bad English, such as "Direct mail is when you send something through . . . ." and "I schedule my campaign in my day planner which really helps you . . . ."
- Non-sentences like "Says Easton."

- Some paragraphs are much too long. One nearly fills a page.
- Bad grammar
- Wrong names
- Michelle recommends submitting a new website address to Inktomi—a defunct search engine which was absorbed by Yahoo back in 2003.
- Michelle says, "Use spell check!" She should.
- Michelle says, "Write a Really Good Book." She should.
- Lack of parallelism
- Asking a question to the reader: "What is your mail routine?" Should readers call Michelle with the answer?
- Missing spaces between words
- Single words that should be plurals
- Michelle recommends that you "sit up straight and smile" during a TELEPHONE interview.
- Michelle recommends that authors have online press kits. Hers has bad grammar, bad typography and obsolete information.
- Using numerals for small numbers—like 3 and 8—but only some of the time
- The "Glossary of Publishing Terms for Author Marketing" contains just seven items. Three of the seven are almost the same and could be combined. One of the seven has nothing to do with marketing and two are not publishing terms. One definition is too narrow. One is inadequate.
- Michelle recommends "free gifts." All gifts are free to the recipient.
- Multiple cases of hyphenating a URL (Uniform Resource Locator, or web address) that does not use a hyphen, making the URL useless

- Publishing a nonworking phone number for her design company
- Recommending a magazine's website and saying "make sure you tell them Michelle Dunn sent you." How do you speak to a website?
- She wrote "ISBN #." That's redundant. Both the "#" and the "N" signify "number."
- Inconsistent use of "http" in URLs
- Michelle says that http://www.uptimebot.com shows backlinks for websites. Actually, it lets you know when your website is unavailable.
- Three out of four items listed as magazines are *not* magazines.
- Her "list" of associations for authors has ONE item.

Michelle emphasizes the need to provide outstanding customer service. This is *not* an issue for most authors since they do not sell books to readers or to booksellers. For most authors, the only important service to provide is writing good books.

Michelle is naive about a writer's relationship with potential readers. She says writers should know where their readers work and if they have children or pets, which movies they see and which magazines they read. Information like this will be difficult, expensive or impossible to obtain on a large scale and will have limited value. Would someone write a book about Winston Churchill any differently if he learned that most potential readers prefer Superman to Batman, or prefer Italian dressing to ranch dressing or don't like beagles?

Michelle presents marketing ideas that are *much too local* for most authors, such as eating in the same restaurants as the target audience. She even recommends buying lunch for prospective book purchasers. That's a good way to go broke.

And, of course, Michelle makes errors in marketing her own book, which is bad for a self-professed marketing expert.

- Amazon identifies CreateSpace, not Michelle's own Never Dunn Publishing, as the publisher.
- Michelle's website and blog are riddled with errors.
- Her blog misses several chances to provide links to order the book.

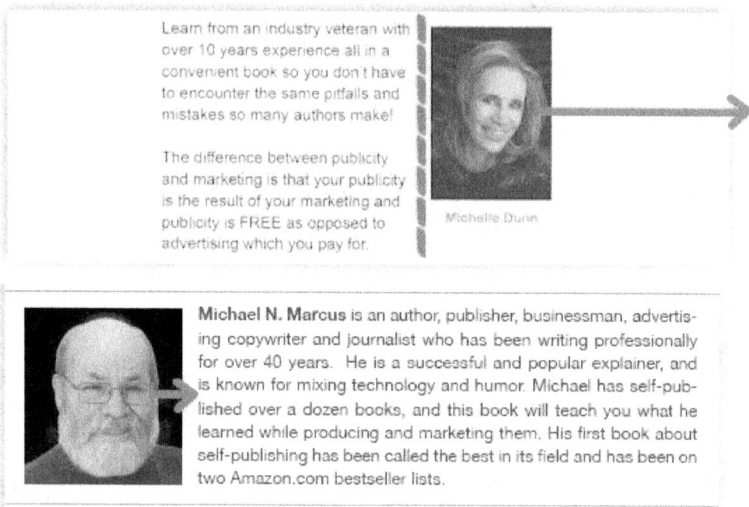

Learn from an industry veteran with over 10 years experience all in a convenient book so you don't have to encounter the same pitfalls and mistakes so many authors make!

The difference between publicity and marketing is that your publicity is the result of your marketing and publicity is FREE as opposed to advertising which you pay for.

Michelle Dunn

Michael N. Marcus is an author, publisher, businessman, advertising copywriter and journalist who has been writing professionally for over 40 years. He is a successful and popular explainer, and is known for mixing technology and humor. Michael has self-published over a dozen books, and this book will teach you what he learned while producing and marketing them. His first book about self-publishing has been called the best in its field and has been on two Amazon.com bestseller lists.

(above) The photo on the back cover shows Michelle leaning *away* from the text. She has turned her back on her own words, visually rejecting what she wrote. She's facing off the cover, and a psychological barrier is created between her and the text.

This is a fundamental design flaw. People tend to look into other people's eyes. Readers tend to be directed by images of faces, eyes or headlights, and readers should not be directed off the page. The lower illustration is from one of my books. Readers see the text while trying to gaze into my eyes. (I'm kidding.) Ironically, there's a nice portrait of Michelle on her website, where she is facing the *right* way.

The second page has both a folio (page number) and a header. Folios and headers do NOT go in the front matter. A professional design company, as WoW! Graphic Designs is supposed to be, should know this. WoW! should also know that headers should not be on the first page of a chapter, that most books should not be set ragged right, that books should not have both indentations and blank pages to indicate the beginning of a paragraph, that a list which appears on the top of a recto page should not have an introduction on the bottom of the preceding verso page, and more. Much more.

I exchanged email and had a phone conversation with Cheryl Microutsicos, owner of WoW! I did not want to criticize her and then find out that she really did not design and lay out the book, or that she started and then someone else completed it. I was hoping she'd say something like, "Please don't mention me. I had nothing to do with that horrible book." But, no, Cheryl did work on the book.

I mentioned the issue of folios and headers in the front matter and Cheryl said, "I really don't know what you're talking about." She said she knows what a header is but not a folio. *Someone who does not know what a folio is should not be involved in publishing.* I wondered if she knows about "verso" and "recto," but was afraid to ask.

Cheryl *can* do good design work, but she simply lacks the education and experience to design books. ("I did not major in book design," she told me.)

Cheryl said she did what the client wanted her to do. This sounds a lot like the Nazi soldiers who were "just following orders" to torture, murder and destroy.

Cheryl wrote me, "I certainly hope the review is based more on the content of the book." Sorry—book reviews can discuss both content and design, especially reviews of books about the book business.

The website for Cheryl's design company shows a concentration on commercial art such as logos. The online "portfolio" shows photos of the blessing of the hounds before a foxhunt.

Not surprisingly, the website has inconsistent typography. Ironically, the WoW! website says, "Just call a professional graphic designer and let them do their magic." Uh-oh!

The WoW! website has strong "testimonials" from seven happy clients. There is exactly ONE testimonial from an author—Michelle Dunn. It says, "Cheryl does high quality work—quickly and professionally. She has helped me with the layout and set up [sic] of my books, book covers, websites, and any promotional materials I need. She goes above and beyond what is expected. I highly recommend her." Since Michelle obviously knows NOTHING about book design, her endorsement means NOTHING.

I am mystified as to why Michelle Dunn chose an unsuitable and distant designer for her books. Perhaps Michelle was impressed by a menu Cheryl designed.

A nice menu is not enough. Book design is a specialty. The experience, taste and computer skills that can produce an attractive menu, website, advertisement, brochure, spec sheet, store sign or birdhouse are NOT sufficient background for designing a book.

Cheryl and her staff have talent—but that's just the beginning. Successful book design requires specific talents plus training, knowledge and experience. I fear for any author who hires WoW! for a book project based on Michelle's recommendation. Disaster awaits.

If Cheryl wants to design another book, I hope she learns how—first. My father advised me never to go to a restaurant until it's been open for a month: "Let them make mistakes with someone *else*," Pop told me. If you're publishing a book, find a designer who has *already* designed good books.

The book has a multitude of errors in what used to be called typesetting. Some errors may be the fault of Michelle, some may be the fault of the editor, and some are the fault of design firm WoW! I can't include them all, but the following list will give you an idea of the scope of the infractions—so maybe you won't repeat the errors.

- Excessive   word   spacing
- Having the title as a header on both verso and recto pages
- Having headers and folios in the front matter
- Repeating the book title on the first TOC page, right below the header that states the title
- The bottom lines in a list are so low that they run into the words below them
- Inconsistent typography in chapter titles
- Bad design: the chapter number and name should be separated or have different typography. Ditto for "part" numbers and names.
- Insufficient hyphenation to lessen the ragged right margin—which should not have been ragged. (below)

#2 – Targeting a niche that is oversaturated. Who is your competition? Get out a notebook and make a list, how long is that list? You will need to narrow down who your book is geared towards or aimed at. If you present your book to an oversaturated market you will have to have some big idea or hook to show why your book is better than all the others. The fewer books on your subject that are out there, the less competition and the better your chances are for success. You can still be successful in an oversaturated market but you have to be clever, have an outstanding hook and be prepared to work harder longer for minimal results.

You can create your niche market by doing some research and finding out specifically who your audience is, what competition is out there and how you are better or different. Once you have that information look at those books and see who their target audience is. Can you narrow down that audience and market to a portion of them? Find small but popular audiences that need what you have where

Michelle wants us to know that "her core values reflect her quest for perfection." The book has hundreds of *imperfections*—errors in writing, editing, design and judgment—which should have been caught by Michelle or her unqualified editor and unqualified designer.

One of Michelle's websites says, "Michelle does everything well, she does it meticulously . . . ." BALONEY!

It also says, ". . . she's driven and ambitious and expects us to do as she does." May God help us.

At $23.95 for just 174 pages of unindexed, sloppy and padded text, the book is *terribly overpriced*. That price is a perfect example of the Yiddish word, "chutzpah." (The traditional example is a man who is on trial for murdering his parents and pleads for mercy on the grounds that he is an orphan.)

The *most important* review on Amazon.com, written by book expert John Culleton, awards Michelle the **minimum one star**.

John wrote, "As a reviewer, a layout artist, an indexer and a publisher I have read dozens of books on publishing and marketing. But for interior layout this book is the worst I have ever seen on any subject. A book for aspiring authors should be an exemplar of proper design and careful execution. This one is full of so many howlers I can't begin to count them. The text is set ragged right. The LCCN and other material that belongs on the copyright page is on the title page. The LCCN isn't an LCCN but rather some other number. There is no index. The ISBN appears nowhere in the front matter. The Glossary has only eight items. The list of useful organizations has only one entry. Part six appears in the TOC but not in the book proper. The list goes on. There is much useful information in this book. But the layout is terrible. Thus I give it just one star."

The *most dangerous* review has **five stars**, and was written by Kathleen Gage.

> She says, "Michelle Dunn has done a great job of compiling solid information on how to market a book. Not just theory, this is practical information any author will benefit from. This is an especially handy guide for any author who is challenged with marketing and selling your books. . . . With everything from laying a solid foundation for marketing, knowing who your target market is, social media marketing, writing press releases, using blogs to market and much more, you can't go wrong with Mosquito Marketing for Authors. The book is a fast read and chock full of great information. I suggest any author who wants great marketing insights get this book today."

It seems like Kathleen ("bestselling author" and "internationally recognized Internet marketing and publicity expert") should be qualified to evaluate a book about marketing books.

So, why is her review dangerous? BECAUSE KATHLEEN WROTE PART OF MICHELLE'S BOOK. She receives promotional benefit from it (and maybe even some money). She is hardly a disinterested third party. Her review is *corrupt* and should be ignored.

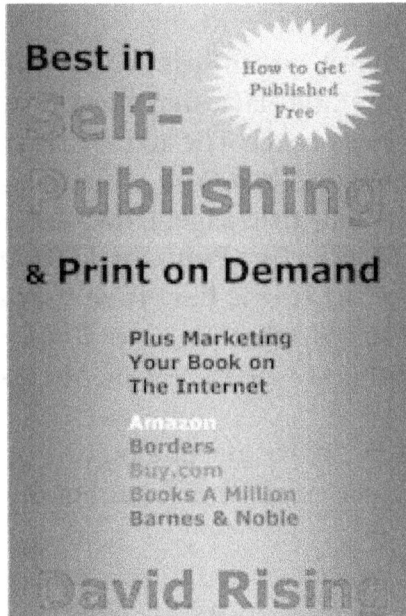

Best in Self-Publishing & Print on Demand
David Rising
Lulu, 2006, 136 pages, $19.95

#3 This is the third-worst book I've ever seen, and a catalog of all of the things you should not do if you write and design a book. It is so crappy that if you use its pages to wipe your behind, you might be dirtier *after* you wipe.

This awful book is titled *Best in Self-Publishing & Print-on-demand,* written by David Rising.

Actually, I'm not sure if *Best in Self-Publishing & Print-on-demand* is the title. That may be just one of two *subtitles* on the ugly, jumbled cover. The actual title could be the deceptive *How to Get Published Free*, which is up at the top of the cover and on the half-title page. However, on page 68, David says the title is *How to Get Published FREE: and Make Money.* Amazon says the title is *Best in Self-Publishing & Print on Demand: Plus Marketing Your Book on the Internet.* That's not the longest title I know of, but it's certainly one of the worst.

David tries to advise authors on self-publishing, but his own book is a great example of what *not* to do.

> delivery   time   is   good   also.   Located   at
> http://www.cafepress.com.   Your   work   might   not   make
> anyone's bestseller list being published here, but it's a good
> place to start especially if you just want to see your work in a
> quality book form. Your book can grow from here and make it
> to the retail chain. I have a journal in this category,
> http://www.cafeshops.com/the_mystical.   If you care to you
> can go to the site for some ideas.

(above) Like many of his inept co-honorees, David eschews hyphens and other devices that could fix the UGH-LEE word spacing in his book. This paragraph indicates that David appreciates "a quality book form." Yeah, right.

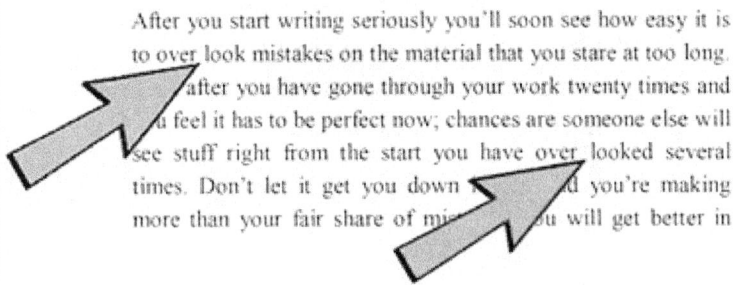

After you start writing seriously you'll soon see how easy it is to over look mistakes on the material that you stare at too long, after you have gone through your work twenty times and u feel it has to be perfect now; chances are someone else will see stuff right from the start you have over looked several times. Don't let it get you down d you're making more than your fair share of mi u will get better in

(above) Appropriately, in a paragraph about overlooking mistakes, David overlooked his misspelling of "overlook" and "overlooked."

David's book is a perfect example of why self-published books are regarded with suspicion by pros in the book industry. Even if the author was too ignorant or too stupid to notice the errors, the publisher, Lulu, should never have let it out the door. But that's too much to expect from Lulu. Lulu's boss says he publishes lots of "really bad books."

- The book is puny (there are just 136 pages), but it has a $19.95 price. Pages 135 and 136 have numbers on them, but nothing else. Maybe David expects his readers to finish writing the book.
- Someone might argue that $19.95 is a fair price, based on the value of what's inside—but only an idiot would make that argument for this book. TWENTY-SEVEN PERCENT consists of instructions for using Lulu to publish a book. The same information is available from Lulu—for free
- There's more unoriginal book padding, including eight pages from Dan Poynter which are available for free on Dan's website and six pages from Audrey Owen which are available for free online. There's also an interview by

Carolyn Campbell which takes up ten pages. It, too, is available as an online freebie. David even reprints unedited advertising for publishing services and presents readers with large blocks of white space and silly pictures that don't relate to the text.

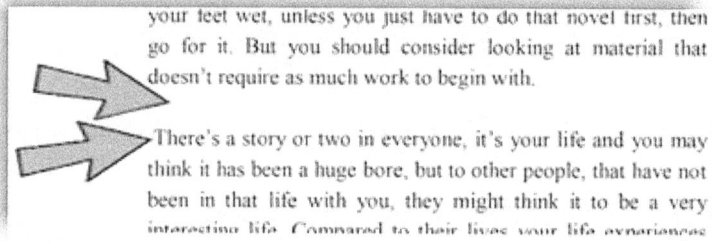

your feet wet, unless you just have to do that novel first, then go for it. But you should consider looking at material that doesn't require as much work to begin with.

There's a story or two in everyone, it's your life and you may think it has been a huge bore, but to other people, that have not been in that life with you, they might think it to be a very interesting life. Compared to their lives, your life experiences

(above) Some book designers like to skip a line between paragraphs. Some prefer to indent the beginning of a paragraph. David does both—or neither.

- In some chapters, both verso and recto pages have identical headers. In some chapters, they have different headers. And, of course, in some chapters there are NO headers. This horrid book has something for everyone.
- Typography is atrocious. Some pages are set justified and some are flush-left and ragged-right—depending on where David copied the text from. Justification is unjust.
- Word spacing is grotesquely ugly.
- (next page) David's rule for spacing between paragraphs is to do whatever he feels like doing at the moment.

Those with a book are treated like an author.

You will also send copies of your book to magazines for review, to book clubs for adoption and to foreign publishers for translation and publication.

Self-Published Books that were "Discovered" by Publishers

- *In Search of Excellence* by Tom Peters. Over 25,000 copies were sold directly to consumers in its first year. Then it was sold to Warner and the publisher sold 10 million more.

- *The Celestine Prophecy* by James Redfield. His manuscript made the rounds of the mainstream houses and then he decided to publish himself. He started by selling copies out of the trunk of his Honda—over 100,000 of them. He subsequently sold out to Warner Books for $800,000. Over 5.5 million copies have been sold.

- *The One-Minute Manager* by Ken Blanchard and Spencer Johnson sold over 20,000 copies locally before they sold out to

- David's writing style is amateurish. His disclaimer speaks to "you, the reader." Who could "you" be *other* than the reader?
- David says, ". . . could result with . . ." It should be "could result in." David believes that an automated spell-checker is a substitute for a copyeditor. It isn't.
- The very first sentence of his introduction has a stupid error: "level playing field for all participates." "Participates" is spelled correctly, but it's the *wrong damned word*.
- David's grammar and sentence structure stink. Here are some examples: "There isn't going to be thousands of

unsold books" and "there is always one or two . . ." and "Don't be afraid you'll not lose anything . . . ."

- He also says, ". . . your writing should at least see the light as for getting published . . ." and "whether you see sells of any significance." I have no idea what the hell he's talking about.
- Another gem is "Unlike a traditional publishing house that can spend huge amounts of money advertising a book they think could be a best seller." There are more examples, but if I typed more, I'd shoot myself. David apparently thinks that any chain of words is a sentence.
- David's spell-checker didn't notice that he left out the second "a" in "manage." Neither did David.
- He spells "subtitle" as "sub title" (two words).

David does give some good advice, such as hiring experts when necessary. Unfortunately, he was too blind, stupid or broke to heed his own advice.

How to get Publish *ed*

(above) David's budget for copyediting was somewhere between zero and nothing.

The index was apparently assembled by a robot and never checked by a homo sapiens or even by a lower primate. An orangutan or even a smart lemur might have done better.

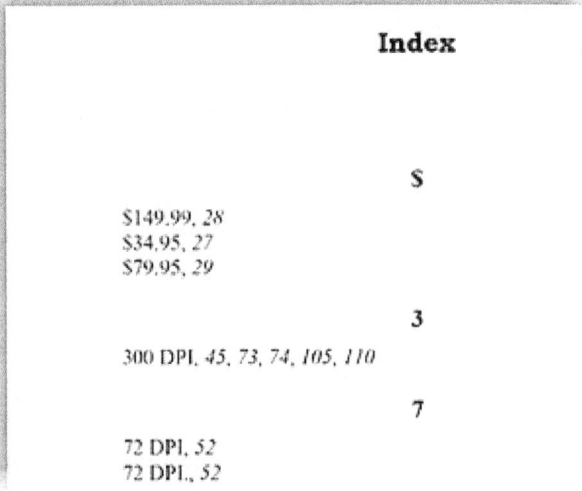

In the index, before the "A" topics, we see topics beginning with $, 3 and 7. The index typography is a strange mix of standard, boldface and underlined text, has no system for capitalization, and uses different fonts. Even email addresses appear in the index and there are terms that no one would ever look for, like "Noah," "hobby" and "private." Expected terms and names are left out. Audrey Owen, who donated a chapter, is *not* listed, but some terms are listed twice. Do we really need 72 DPI as well as 72 DPI with a period after it?

- The ghastly front cover screams, "How to Get Published Free." The word "free" is *not* indexed, and I couldn't find anything about free publishing inside the book.
- The sloppy and poorly written back cover says, "This book will explain to you how to use database logic . . . ."

David also says, "Understanding database logic will be a key ingredient to having any success marketing . . . ." The section on database logic discusses book titles, keywords (and "key words"—David spells it both ways in the same paragraph) and has some incomprehensible drivel about Barnes & Noble and Amazon, but NO-WHERE DOES DAVID EXPLAIN what database logic is.

- David recommends investing in inventory so you can sell books through Amazon's "Marketplace" in competition with Amazon itself. He claims, "When a book first goes on sale they will have a very limited supply of books and it can take up to 13 days before a book is shipped." That's not true.

- David says, "Lulu only charges you 20% commission on your profits. So, for any product you sell on the site you get 80% profit." David should have said "80% OF THE profit," not "80% profit." That can be a huge difference. The word "only," by the way, should follow "charges you."

This is the only book I recall that says nothing about its author. Maybe that's because there is *nothing* in David's education or experience that qualifies him to write about the topic. David's website says nothing about his writing experience, either.

I'm a strong supporter of freedom of the press. Until now, I've firmly believed that any writer should be able to publish anything. However, after buying this slim and nearly worthless volume, I might be willing to consider a licensing requirement for writers. I have no doubt that David would fail the test.

The book looks like it was designed by someone who is blind, edited by someone who is illiterate and published by a company with no standards. Basically, it's expensive toilet paper with an ugly cover—sort of a *MAD* magazine parody, intended to point out the dangers of ignorant and inept publishing.

I bought the third edition, published in July, 2006. It's very disturbing to contemplate how bad the first two editions were. Since there have been no updates in five years, apparently David finally got some sense—and ended his writing career.

Unfortunately, based on Amazon.com reviews (and there has been not even one review per year), a few people bought this disastrous book and relied on it to get into publishing.

One realistic review:

> "If this book is its own example of self-publishing, then don't do it - at least not with the company he recommends. The book was poorly written in places and in other places poorly laid out, even to the point of repeated paragraphs and aborted lines resumed after a gap of several lines. Even a mediocre copy editor would have helped."

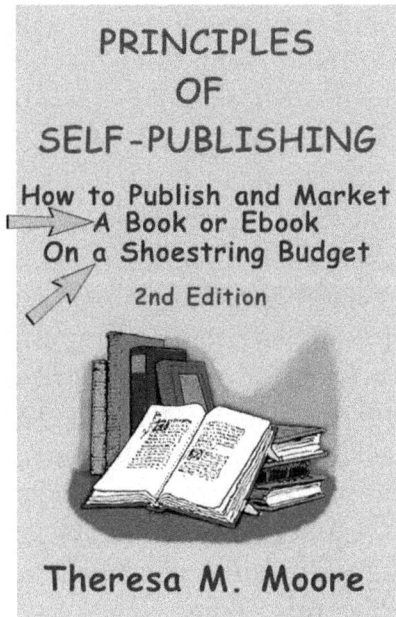

PRINCIPLES
OF
SELF-PUBLISHING

How to Publish and Market
A Book or Ebook
On a Shoestring Budget

2nd Edition

Theresa M. Moore

Principles of Self-Publishing: How to Publish and Market A Book or Ebook On a Shoestring Budget (2 nd edition)
Theresa A. Moore
CreateSpace, 2010, 152 pages, $15.95

#4 **The fourth-worst is a really bad 152-page book about publishing. The material in it could have been used to print a few decent eight-page booklets.**

Unlike MS. ELIYZABETH YANNE STRONG-ANDERSON, who types in uppercase only, and is our first-place loser, Theresa M. Moore is coherent, experienced and apparently sane.

Her problems are that she is extremely careless, knows less than she thinks she knows, has an unjustifiably high opinion of her own editing ability and frequently ignores her own advice.

Theresa's *Principles of Self-Publishing: How to Publish and Market A Book or Ebook On a Shoestring Budget* is one of an increasing number of books about self-publishing written by people who are poorly equipped to teach the subject.

Theresa has apparently had some success writing books in the fantasy and sci-fi genres. She says that she has 30 years of experience as a writer, illustrator and publisher. She's a member of the Count Dracula Society and has an AA degree with a major in accounting and a minor in advertising design. Sadly, her experience with vampire fangs, debits and paste-ups does *not* qualify her to instruct others in book publishing.

Theresa says, "I succeeded at producing books that are just as good in quality as those of the big house publishers. All it takes is dedication and the will to learn, and you too can be a successful author in a matter of a few days." Theresa has a fatal blend of ignorance, inattention and egomania. Her book includes multiple errors that self-publishing authors should avoid. **Theresa produced a very bad book and she provides very bad advice.**

Some of her errors:

- The cover looks childish and is badly edited. It is *really* ugly, with an illustration by the author that looks like fifty-cent clip art. The typeface resembles something a third-grader would scrawl on the blackboard. According to Theresa, the title's typeface should be "attention grabbing." The face she chose is sleep-inducing—or barf-inducing.

- Instead of a title and subtitle, the book seems to have two titles. The main title is dull enough to induce a coma. I doubt that many people buy books with "Principles Of" in the title—unless commanded to do so by a professor. Theresa wisely says, "No book is complete without a great title." Therefore, her book is *not* complete.

- The subtitle does a much better selling job, but has some silly errors. It has both uppercase and lowercase versions of the word "A." It uses lowercase for "or" but uppercase for "on." When I questioned the author about this, she said these were deliberate decisions, not errors, and "It makes the subtitle easier to read." No it doesn't.

- The type on the spine is light pink-brown. It's tiny type, and fades into the pea-soup-green background color. If you look closely, you'll see the same inconsistent typography as on the front cover. The title page also has the inconsistent typography, but strangely omits "or ebook" from the subtitle. The copyright page, too, has the weird typography and also leaves out part of the subtitle. Like the rest of the book, the copyright page eschews hyphens, and has very ugly word spacing. It shows "2009, 2010" and "2009,2010"—one sequence *with* and one *without* a space after the comma. Someone should have noticed these errors before printing.

- The back cover repeats the same homemade illustration and childlike typeface. It has a copyright notice, which I've never before seen on a book cover.

- Theresa tells us that she disliked the smell of rubber cement but loved the smell of mimeograph ink. She says, "It smelled so scholastic." Maybe her inhalation of

49

glue and ink fumes hurt her ability to discern and correct errors in books. Be careful about what you sniff.

- After mentioning the ink, she wrote, "But I digress." Unfortunately, the very slim book is *filled* with silly digressions and unimportant information.
- Theresa says, "The ebook *was developed was developed for . . . .*" Someone should have noticed the repetition before printing.

The Elements of Editing : *A Modern Guide for Editors and Journalists* by Arthur Plotnik.

Above is a typical and tragic example of the ugly word spacing that occurs when Theresa uses full justification but refuses to hyphenate—like too many other amateur publishers. Her pages have excessive word spacing, plus rivers, widows and orphans, and waste paper. It's OK to skip hyphens on a website or in an e-book, but hyphens *are* important in print.

When I mentioned the problems caused by her lack of hyphenation, Theresa responded, "I don't know what you are referring to. My proof copies do not look that way. This may be a printer artifact, and since my service uses several outside sources to print once the book is sold I have no control over that either." That response demonstrates Theresa's characteristic ignorance which contradicts her touted experience. A digital printing press *does not change word spacing*. In fact, it *cannot* change word spacing. Ugly pages are ugly even when viewed as a Microsoft Word document or an Adobe PDF.

- Sloppiness is abundant. On the first page after the introduction, a comma is missing, "Christian" is spelled with a lowercase "c" and a word is missing. These lapses are on just *one* page, and are an unfortunate precursor of errors to come.

- The book is consistently inconsistent, with variations in spelling, capitalization and punctuation.
- We're told that Lulu is "based" in North Carolina but CreateSpace is "base" in California.
- Oddly enough, Theresa prefers the British spelling of "grey" to the American "gray." Gray is a color. Grey is a colour. She also uses the British meaning of "blurb," and the Brit style of putting a period *after* a closing quotation mark—at least some of the time.
- She says, ". . . your work will be read by others who may have the expertise you do not. They will be highly critical of your work if you cannot justify your theories with the facts to support them." Theresa is absolutely right.
- She says, "People who read books usually do not read blogs, and vice versa." I doubt that Theresa has facts to support this silly theory. Lots of people read *both* blogs *and* books. Some people read blogs *about* books.
- Theresa puts "only" before verbs and gerunds when they should be *after* them.
- There are awkward phrases, like "I used to use . . . ."
- Theresa wrote, ". . . write to engage the reader's interest and entertainment." How does a writer engage a reader's entertainment?
- She advises authors to ". . . go over the whole thing and weed out the mistakes." In the very next sentence she typed "everytime" instead of "every time." "Everytime" is a song sung by Britney Spears, but is *not standard English*. Maybe Theresa was thinking of "everyone," which *is* one word.

- Theresa says it's OK to use the same title that another book uses. While titles can't be copyrighted, elements in titles can be trademarked, and it's stupid to take the deliberate risk of losing sales, confusing potential buyers and possibly being sued for trademark infringement.
- She thinks that PDF stands for "portable document file." The real meaning is portable document FORMAT. It's possible to have a PDF file, but not a PD *file file*.
- She typed "ISBN number." That's redundant, because the "N" stands for "number."

BARNES&NOBLE
978-0983057246

amazon.com®
978-0983057246

Those numbers look the same to me.

Theresa Writes, "The last number [in ISBNs] may be different on several bookselling sites owing to a check digit for inventory control." That's *not true*. The check digit is provided by the ISBN agency (Bowker in the USA) to ensure that the other digits are correct. The check digit has *nothing to do with inventory control*. Booksellers may use their own stock numbers, but booksellers *do not* alter the ISBN assigned to a book.

will take 65% of whatever you set. The rest is profit. Beginning in July of 2010 Amazon will take only 30% of the retail price of ebooks priced at $9.99 or less, so it is to your advantage to set your ebooks to a reasonable price in line with what similar books in the Amazon marketplace will sell for.

The paragraph above has an ugly orphan which could easily have been eliminated. The book is *filled* with orphans, widows and rivers. Someone with 30 years' experience in publishing and advertising should have known enough to have removed them. Theresa said these defects were caused by the printer. She's *wrong*.

- Theresa provides an extensive section on antitrust laws. It's interesting, but hardly necessary for self-publishers. I'll label it "padding."
- There's also an extensive section on HTML (HyperText Markup Language) and building a website. Authors need websites, but they don't need to know HTML. This section is padding, too.
- The book has a page about advertising in newspapers and magazines. That's a waste of a publisher's money, and a wasted page in this slim book.
- There's a long, dull, boring, sleep-inducing, unnecessary, page-wasting section on bookkeeping that few self-publishers are likely to need or to be interested in. They don't need to know about amortization or inventory control. This is more padding—in a very thin book.
- Theresa provides OVER FORTY PAGES about bookkeeping, pricing and taxes—an awfully big chunk of a 152-page book about publishing!
- The book has a section on stress reduction, sleep, exercise, avoiding stimulants, Feng Shui and self-esteem. This information is mostly useless, and contributes to the unnecessary padding. In this section, she advises

writers to ". . . keep a supply of small snacks, water, and a period of nap time by your side." Does the nap time go on your chair, on your desk, on the floor or does it hang on the wall? An editor should have caught this!

- She has several strings of words that begin with upper-case words and end with periods—but there are no verbs, so they're *not sentences.*
- Theresa eschews "self-publishing company" in favor of "self-help publisher." The world really doesn't need another synonym for "self-publishing company," and "self-help publisher" has a different meaning from what she intends: it's a publisher of self-help books.
- Theresa says that "Lulu or CreateSpace will offer you a basic designer which will . . . ." A designer is a "who," not a "which."
- Theresa wants us to resize photos "to fit the text area at 90 to 100%." There's nothing wrong with 30% or 60% or any percentage that provides the proper image size.
- The book's subtitle emphasizes "a shoestring budget," but Theresa's cheapo design decisions have led to an UGH-LEE book.
- She also saved money by not hiring an editor who should have caught the abundant mistakes. I asked her if she self-edited and she answered, "Of course. I have edited many others' books myself." Based on her own book, I feel sorry for her clients. Also, *no one* should be her own editor. Even a professional editor who writes books needs to hire an editor. If you can't afford to hire an editor, you can't afford to publish a book.
- Theresa writes, "I edited my stories as many as fifteen times before I am satisfied that it is good enough to publish." Maybe if Theresa read *that* sentence sixteen times, she would have fixed the tenses and the subject-verb agreement. If she read the book seventeen times,

maybe she would have noticed that the paragraph is missing its indentation. Sadly, even if she read the book one hundred times, she probably would not have noticed how ugly it is.

- When I asked her why she did not hyphenate, Theresa responded, "Word processing software typically justifies when set that way. Why hyphenate when the whole word will be sent to the next line? This is not Linotype letter die setting." That's *baloney*. Her book was made unnecessarily ugly because she refused to hyphenate. The term "letter die setting" does not appear in either Google or Bing, and Theresa *refused* to explain what she meant by it.

- I asked her, "Why didn't you provide an index? It's unusual for a nonfiction how-to book not to have an index." She said, "Many people using the book do not look at an index, nor care to." An index *is* useful, and many readers expect to find one in a how-to book. Sadly, Theresa was being either lazy or cheap—or both.

- Theresa tells us: "Criticism helps you to see the things you missed because you are editing inside your own head. What you think is a brilliant idea may turn out to be a real clunker . . . ." Her entire book is a real clunker.

Principles of Self-Publishing

public. But I was not sure which direction to go and there were very few resources. Companies like Microsoft® and Apple® were working on improving and expanding the storage capacity of their computers, but not many people owned their own computers yet. Google and Yahoo did not exist yet. Netscape was a burbling infant crawling on the floor. BlackBerry

(above) Theresa tries to limit her printing cost by using the minimum amount of paper. In the example shown, the header

is much too close to the first line of text. The page's upper, lower and outside margins are too small. On the other hand, the inside "gutter" margin is too large for this thin, perfect-bound book.

Some of her bad advice:

- Theresa says that a back cover's margins "are the mirror image of the front." There is *no* reason for them to be mirror images of each other, as long as they meet the printer's requirements. She also says that the back cover can be "completely blank." That's true if you are going to give books away or sell them yourself. If you want booksellers to sell them for you, the back cover needs an ISBN and barcode.
- Our ignorant expert says that the county where your business is located "will require you to post the registration [of your business] on your own in your local newspaper." That's not true in many counties.
- In her inappropriate role of legal advisor, Theresa advises us that the abbreviation for Limited Partnership is "Ltd." Actually, the correct abbreviation is "LP." "Ltd." is the abbreviation for "Limited"—the U.K. equivalent of an American corporation where shareholders have limited liability.
- She says that self-publishers "must obtain a tax permit or resale certificate." If you or your company are not selling books, you don't need to get involved with sales tax. If you ship books only out of your home state to a state where you have no physical presence ("nexus"), you don't need to collect or remit sales tax, although this policy may change in the future.
- The math non-whiz tells us that "As the price of your book goes up, the demand for it will go down." That's

true, in theory. And then she adds, "Your costs will go up as the demand for it goes up." Huh? With POD, the cost of printing each book may go down a bit if you order 50 or more at once, but *does not go up*. With offset printing, quantity discounts can be substantial.

- Theresa tells us that Lightning Source "will insert a generic barcode to your cover if you do not have one, but prefers you already have one." That's *not* true. Lightning is perfectly happy to provide a cover template with a *custom* barcode to correspond to your ISBN, and it's FREE. A generic barcode would be *useless*. A book's barcode *must* correspond to its ISBN.

- The non-expert tells us that type size is "presented in points per inch." That's wrong. Type size is expressed in points, but *not* per inch. Maybe she was thinking of "dots per inch." In modern typography, one point is 1/72nd of an inch, so there are 72 points per inch. Someone with 30 years' experience in publishing and advertising should know this.

- In a discussion of page margins, Theresa suggests "usually 1/2 or .5 inch all around." Grade school was long ago, but I'm pretty sure that 1/2 inch and .5 inch are THE SAME THING, and that either one is *too small* for a book margin. The basic rule of thumb is that you should be able to hold the book in your hands without your thumbs covering any text. Adult human thumbs are usually wider than half an inch.

- Theresa offers this silly rule: "Never use a TIF file when a JPG will do." That's bad advice. In many cases, when a JPG file is saved, it loses some detail. A TIF file is "lossless." She says that most publishers prefer JPGs. Don't believe her. Besides, her book is supposedly written for self-publishers who will be dealing with printers—*not* with other publishers.

- She says that the number of pages in a book must be even *or* divisible by four. If a number is divisible by four, it *is* an even number. Actually, the proper number depends on the printing equipment, varies from company to company and may change over time.
- According to Theresa, the title page should be the first page in a book. In many books, the first page—or pages—have comments ("blurbs") from reviewers or casual readers. Many books use a "half title" (or "bastard title") page ahead of the title page.
- Theresa is concerned about the cost of paper. She tells us, "As the price of printing goes up due to market and paper supply issues, the greatest amount of information must fit the smallest space." Actually, POD prices have been stable for at least three years and Theresa's effort to save paper results in really ugly pages. This is the only book I've ever seen that has chapters ending and beginning on the *same* page. The back of the book has five blank pages. If Theresa did some simple arithmetic, those pages could have carried information and/or allowed more attractive pages, adding just a few cents to the cost of printing the book.
- In one of Theresa's worst errors, she says that Lightning Source "is a full service publisher." Lightning is *not* a publisher of any kind. It is a printing house that works for publishers. It does NOT provide services such as editing and page formatting, which a self-publishing company provides. Anyone who is advising publishers should know the difference between a printer and a publisher.
- Theresa complains that Lightning Source charges an "exhorbitant shipping fee" for a proof. Both her spelling and her assessment are wrong. Actually, $30 is not bad for printing the proof and next-day shipping.

- In discussing Lulu, Theresa says, ". . . you will have to purchase their free distribution package." How does someone purchase something that's free?
- She tells us that "CreateSpace also does absolutely nothing to help you promote your book, to Amazon or anywhere else. They have a shopping cart and that is all, and they are the publisher of record on Amazon." This is *all wrong*. If you publish through CreateSpace ("CS"), your book is automatically available on Amazon, with "look inside the book" included. CS is *not* the publisher of record unless you want it to be. CS is perfectly willing to print a publisher's name, logo and ISBN on books—including the book you are now reading.
- Theresa faults CreateSpace for not accepting PayPal payments and lauds Lulu for accepting PayPal. It's hard to believe that anyone without at least one credit card would go into the publishing business.
- **Here's some of the absolute worst publishing advice I've encountered anywhere:** "Concentrate on selling your books from your own web site and you will do better than if you rely on others for your sales." That's *irresponsible and untrue*. Booksellers' websites like Amazon.com get thousands of times the traffic of any self-pubber's website. It's silly for an author to get involved with running a warehouse and shipping department and handling credit cards. I bought my copy of Theresa's book from Amazon—not from Theresa's website.
- Theresa wants self-publishers to sell books, but warns against having phone numbers on sales sites. That's stupid. Lots of shoppers need information or prefer to order by phone. She warns that telemarketers may call in the middle of the night. If you work from home, you should have different phone numbers for business and

personal use. There is no need to have the business line ring after hours—and certainly no need to answer late-night calls. That's what voicemail is for.

- In addition to being wrong about "PDF," Theresa is also wrong about "LCCN." It stands for Library of Congress *Control* Number—not *Certification* Number. She says there is a "small fee" for an LCCN. There is *no fee*. She says you need to send at least two copies of your book to get an LCCN. One copy is enough.

- She talks about preparing a query letter and submitting a manuscript to a publisher. Those topics *don't* belong in a book for self-publishers.

- Theresa cautions authors not to blog "too much" because it takes time away from book writing. She does not explain how much *is* too much. Besides, blogging can promote book sales, and material written for a blog can be used for books—like this one.

- The ignorant author tells us, "Some online booksellers, like Amazon, take 60 to 65% [of the cover price]. I kid you not." Theresa may not be kidding, but she's *way* off base. Amazon is willing to collect 20%—or even just 10% when it discounts a book.

- Theresa is very wrong when she tells us, "In the book world, you must always round UP to the nearest dollar less five cents or a penny, so your book's list price can be $17.95 or $17.99." While most cover prices end in 95 cents, that's a custom—not a requirement.

- Theresa says, "The suggested retail or list price . . . is the maximum a seller may charge for the book new." Actually, many booksellers offer books for substantially *more* than the list ("cover") prices.

- She also tells us that "The list price is often set as the perceived value of the book on the marketplace." It's up to a buyer—*not* the publisher or bookseller—to perceive a value. Theresa perceives the value of her book to be $15.95. I paid $15.95, but, after reading it, I perceived the value to be about two bucks.

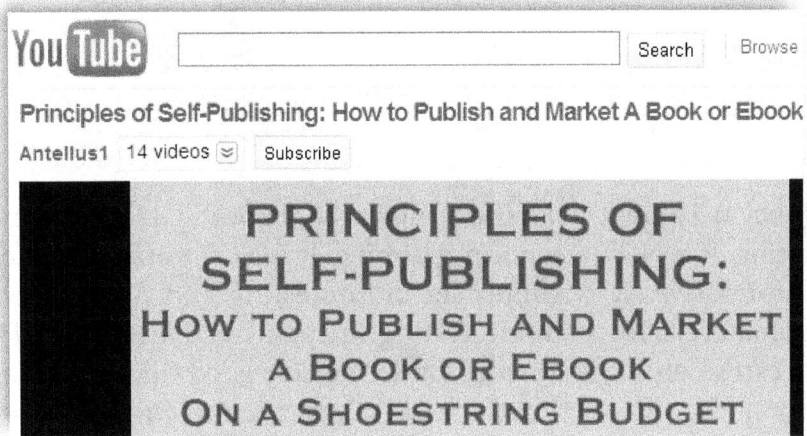

Theresa is a big believer in promotional videos, but they're useless unless you can find a way to make people watch them. Her own video is *awful*, and I don't mean awe-inspiring.

The book includes instructions for making a simple "slide show" video for YouTube. She says, "If you are a complete novice at this here is where I can help you make a simple video that will do more to help you market your book than anything else you might do. The press release is effective but the video has more reach. You can make it as exciting and attention grabbing as the best movie trailer on the planet. The better you make it, the more people who will be inclined to watch it . . . ."

The basic rules of editing and preparation of a manuscript, and how to present it to the right people.

(above) Theresa's video is as ugly as her book is. It is NOT exciting. It is NOT attention-grabbing. It is NOT entertaining or informative. It is simply an uninteresting and unattractive commercial for an uninteresting and unattractive book, and it is extremely unlikely to go viral. The *only* good thing I can say about the video is that the letter A's on the opening screen are consistent—unlike the A's on the book cover.

OK, it's time for a compliment: Theresa provides some good instruction for writing fiction.

Theresa knows a lot—but not nearly enough to teach about publishing. Even sadder, she does not follow the advice she provides for others. That is inexcusable.

Another compliment: Theresa provides some wise advice: "pay close attention to every part of the publishing process, including the preparation and presentation of the manuscript."

It's a shame that she did not pay attention to her own advice. Stay away from her book—except to learn what *not* to do.

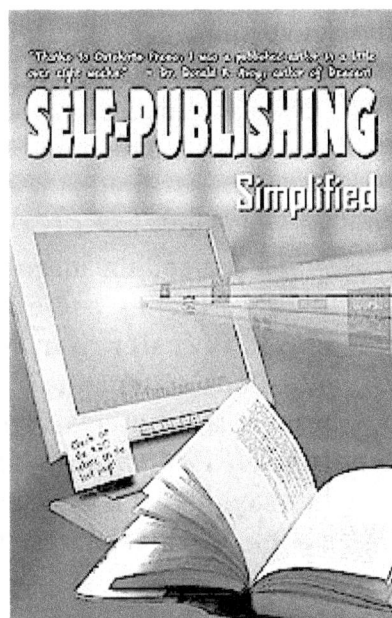

Self-Publishing Simplified
Brent Sampson
Outskirts Press, 2005, 110 pages, $5.95

#5

This book is ranked fifth-worst. It's small, but errors are abundant. The author is a book publisher who *badly* needs a book editor.

The fifth-worst book I've found is *Self Publishing Simplified*, written by Brent Sampson, the head of self-publishing company Outskirts Press. His ineptitude and misrepresentation have won him a prime place in the Publishing Hall of Shame. The book is *particularly* bad because Brent is a publisher, has a college degree in English and claims to be both an "expert in the field of publishing" and a bestselling author.

Here's what was above Brent's name in a press release: "**Now publishing a book is easier than reading one . . . .**" Not only is that a ridiculous statement, it also makes Brent seem extra-stupid, because the sentence continues: "**. . . if you happen to be reading *Self-Publishing Simplified*. . . .**"Brent wrote that book, so he's saying that it's harder to *read* his book than it is to *publish* a book. Wow! If he wasn't the boss, he'd be fired for this bit of idiocy.

Brent's personal website has a stupid error: "earn up to tens-of-thousands a dollars." Brent urges writers to use an editor and he says, "Errors in your writing cause readers to question your credibility." I question his.

Outskirts Press's publishing packages include editing services, but the company's own publications need much better editing. The *Simplified* book functions as an advertisement for Brent's company, but it's filled with embarrassing errors. Apparently, no one was willing to tell the boss that he screwed up. Or maybe Brent is such an egomaniac that he saw no need for editing or fact checking. His wife was an English major, too. She could have helped—if he asked her

- The book has a foreword written by Brent—which goes against the normal book-publishing rules that any publisher *should* know. Forewords are not supposed to be written by the author. Brent should have called that section a "preface" or an "introduction" or hired someone else to write a foreword.

- On five pages, Brent refers to "off-set" printing, with a hyphen between the "off" and the "set." That's a really stupid error, especially coming from a book publisher. The correct term is "offset," and it's been that way for over 100 years, since offset printing was invented.

- According to Brent, "Peter Mark first published the *Thesaurus* in 1852," strangely ignoring the much more famous Peter Roget who published *his* Thesaurus in the same year. Actually, "Mark" was Peter Mark Roget's *middle* name, so Brent is two-thirds right. That's *not* good enough.

- He says getting an ISBN is a "headache." **That's just not true.** You can easily order ten ISBNs in about five minutes. All you need is a computer and a credit card. No Tylenol is necessary.

- Brent talks about troubles that "most self-published authors" have with getting their books distributed, the high percentages paid to Amazon, and the high costs of setting up websites. **This not true.** It's all self-serving fiction designed to make Outskirts look good.
    1. Brent can't possibly know the experiences of "most self-published authors."
    2. Book distribution can be easy and trouble-free.
    3. Amazon accepts a small percentage.
    4. A website can be set up for very little money.

- Brent says that, with independent self-publishing, you "undergo the arduous task of starting a publishing company on your own in order to print, distribute, and market it." **That's just not true.** It's not arduous. If it was arduous, few people would do it. Very few self-publishers own a printing press or delivery truck.

- Brent wants readers to believe that "The disadvantage [of independent self-publishing] is that it is time-consuming and very risky to self-publish a book by yourself, due to the up-front financial investment." **That's just not true.** The up-front financial investment can be just a few hundred bucks. $1,000 is more realistic, and not much of a burden. Brent's customers can pay over $6,000 to get published and promoted.

A self-publisher's book warehouse?

- Brent says independent self-publishers "are left with thousands of unsold copies and without an effective way of getting their books into the hands of readers," and "The independently self published authors I know all have boxes of books in their garage and park their cars on the street." **That's just not true.** Apparently Brent knows the wrong people. He certainly doesn't know me. My garage is not filled with books. I want to write and market books, not operate a warehouse.

- He also insists, "Distributors rarely work with one-time authors, so once you have books printed, you may find it challenging to move them from your garage and into the hands of readers." **That's just not true**. Ingram Book Group is the biggest book wholesaler in the United States, and it distributes many titles from one-time authors whose books are printed on demand.

- Brent says, "If you have the money to invest (usually $10,000 or so) and the time to invest (usually 20 hours a week), and the ability (are you an editor, designer, accountant, publicist, and website designer?), then publishing your book independently may be the proper path for you. It's not just an adventure, it's a job!" **More lies**. The $10,000 figure is five to ten times too high. An author should not be the editor, and can easily hire a designer and an accountant. Many authors can do their own publicity and design their own websites. The time spent each week can vary tremendously.

Brent Sampson's silly errors and outright deceptions do not inspire confidence. This book has a $5.95 cover price. That's five bucks too much. Used copies are on sale for a penny each. That's fair.

If, for some strange reason, you actually trust Brent's knowledge and opinions, he'll be glad to give you personal advice on the phone—for $250 per hour.

He's also available for hire as a public speaker. He lists "Independent self-publishing vs. print-on-demand. What's the difference?" as one of his topics. I'd love to hear him explain that—but I wouldn't pay to hear it.

I'm an independent self-publisher and I use print on demand. They're not incompatible or opposites. Brent's topic is like asking "What's the difference between a car and an engine?"—a question that does not have to be asked or answered.

Brent offers readers much misinformation. He makes in-dependent self-publishing seem much harder than it really is, and he wants readers to believe that he knows the experiences of most self-published authors.

The back-of-book bio says that Brent is an "accomplished artist and writer." I'm not impressed with his writing accomplishments.

A personal memo to Brent: Not only were you wrong about "off-set" vs. "offset." You're also wrong about "to whit." The correct phrase is "to wit." And, in your bio, the final phrase "one of the fastest growing on-demand publishing companies in America" should come after "Outskirts Press," not after "2002." And, while you're at it, fix the misspelled "importantly" on your website.

Even publishers need editors. If Brent used one of the Out-skirts editors, either the editor is unsuited to the job, or is afraid to correct the boss. Maybe both.

Some reviews from Amazon.com:

> "As someone who has self-published over 30 books, I can honestly say that this book is not worth reading."

> "Like reading an infomercial. If you want to know how to self-publish a book with Outskirts Press, and you're too lazy to get the information from their website, this is the book for you. I expected more on the nuts and bolts of self publishing; after all, the title does lead one to think this. Oh well. On the plus side, it wasn't too expensive."

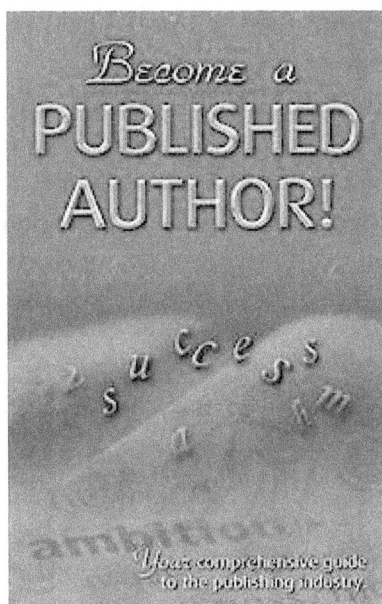

Become a Published Author!
Dave Giorgio
Infinity Publishing, 2009, 95 pages, $14.95

#6 **The sixth worst "book" is another ad masquerading as a book. It has some useful information, but is very poorly produced and terribly out-of-date. It's supposed to attract potential author customers. It's more likely to drive them away.**

Infinity Publishing produced a small book called *Become a Published Author!*, aimed at prospective customers. It explains how Infinity operates and includes useful information about preparing a manuscript for publication. The book has another purpose: to seduce writers into becoming customers by providing a sample of a book that Infinity has published. Ironically and stupidly, the book is really ugly, inside and out. After more than nine years, the book has *just one* Amazon review.

The 90-page book has a phony cover price of $14.95 that no one ever pays. Infinity gives it away for free. Independent sellers on Amazon.com offer new copies for 50 cents, and used ones for a penny! The book is probably worth a penny.

The cover has very little contrast between the text and a weird illustration that looks like the interior of a cadaver with letters sprinkled on it. The subtitle is *A complete guide to Infinity Publishing's "just in Time" Book Publishing Method.*

"Just-in-time" should be hyphenated. "Time Book Publishing Method" should not have initial capital letters. A publisher should know this. So should an editor. It's a bad idea to make dumb mistakes on the cover of an important book which you hope will win business.

Book critics have complained that companies such as Lulu never look at the books they churn out. Lulu and its competitors assume that, if the author customer approves a book, it's good enough to print.

As irresponsible as that attitude is, what Infinity has done is even worse. Infinity's bosses apparently did not take a good look at a book *their own employees* put together to represent the company's best work.

The book says that "We only publish high quality books," that Infinity "provides buyers with a beautiful product," and "As you hold this book in your hands, take note of the quality of the printing . . . ." If you take note, you should be horrified because of the bad book quality *and* bad grammar. The first brief statement should say: "We publish only high-quality books." A publisher of high-quality books should know better.

Each tii

sale (r

find   quarterl

(above) The tops and bottoms of some facing pages are badly misaligned. The page margins are considerably smaller than in a standard book.

If this book is an example of Infinity's best work—the *sample* they use to attract new business—imagine how bad their *regular* books are.

Optional Add-on Services:

Copyediting: We can copyedit your book for grammar, spelling, and punctuation errors for a cost of $.013 per word.

(above) Infinity will be glad to sell you copyediting services.

(below) Look at the blooper the editors did not notice, in at least *three* editions of the book. A book this important should be *free of errors*. The Infinity website has errors, like "in to" instead of "into." Where are the copyeditors?

Price change: Once your book is published, we recommend that you do not change its price. If you do, you will be charged $200. Due to of the time it takes for other databases to catch up with such a change, your book could sell for different prices for a while.

To dig its grave even deeper, Infinity brags that it has invested millions in printing equipment. It says, "Most of our competitors . . . involve a third party to print and ship books, yielding lower quality and less reliable fulfillment."

Infinity offers an optional program to distribute books through Ingram Book Group, with printing by Ingram's Lightning Source division.

Infinity claims that "While their books are not as high quality as ours, they're considered acceptable." That's not true. Many independent self-publishers, most of Infinity's competitors and many major traditional publishers use Lightning and Ingram—with *no* quality or fulfillment problems.

The book's size is just 5.5×8.5 inches —smaller than the standard 6×9-inch size for similar books. Strangely, Infinity can't print 6×9 books. The company lies that that "Most of our competitors can produce only 5.5"×8.5" books."

Infinity brags about being the only company that can print an 8 X 8 book. Big deal! The 8×8 size is good for family photo books, but, for most writers, 6×9 is much more important. Infinity claims that it offers "the most freedom and best value of any publisher hands down." If it can't produce a common 6×9 book, how much "freedom" do you have?

The book says that Infinity sells books to its authors with a 40% discount off list price and that "Our competitors sell you your book at 25% off (if you are lucky)." That's not true. Outskirts Press offers discounts up to 48%. Wheatmark's author discount is 40%. The discount at iUniverse can be as much as 65%.

My version of the book was published in February 2009 and is *badly* out-of-date. It discusses saving files onto floppy discs or a Zip disc and provides instructions on composing a book with the ancient year-2000 version of Microsoft Word.

(below) Should we believe Infinity's book—or its website?

We sell only printed books (not digital or downloadable books) because nothing compares to the real thing. Digital e-books are too easily pirated off the Internet, resulting in lost royalties for you. They are also too difficult to read. Try to read just five pages of any wordy document on your computer. As your eyes strain and your neck starts to cramp, imagine how readers of your book would feel. Wouldn't this ruin the experience of reading your book? And of course, you can't curl up with a computer the way you can with a good book.

In fact, Barnes & Noble stopped selling e-books — a telling sign.

INFINITELY ENJOYABLE
Your book on iPad, Kindle, nook and more!

You asked, we responded. And as you'd expect, our foray into eBook publishing is comprehensive, high quality, and GUARANTEED.

You've seen and read about the eBook format. Whether via Apple's iPad or Amazon's Kindle, there's a legitimate new platform for reading. We are proud to offer eBook publishing with the best feature set in the industry.

The book says, "We sell only printed books (not digital or downloadable books) because nothing compares to the real thing." It strongly criticizes the difficulty and the physical pain caused by reading e-books. Infinity warns us that e-books ruin the reading experience, and says, "Barnes & Noble stopped selling e-books—a telling sign." B&N may have stopped selling e-books at one point, but now expects them to be the savior of the company.

High up on the homepage of Infinity's website is this message: "We now offer the complete eBook Publishing solution."

Apparently they realize that the warnings in the 2009 book are baloney. Or, even if reading e-books does cause eye strain and neck cramps, those are not reasons for the company to turn down a possible source of revenue, and to have a policy that makes Infinity uncompetitive.

- Strangely, the book I received in 2010 is version 3.5, with a copyright date of 2009, and a notice that it was published in February, 2009.
- I also have a copy of another version 3.5, with a copyright date of 2007 and a notice that it was published in November, 2007.
- I downloaded what should be the latest version of the book—the one that Infinity wants prospective customers to read. This book is also version 3.5, copyrighted in 2008, and published in July, 2008. Yes—the download is older than the physical book that was distributed 19 months earlier!
- There are slight differences among the three 3.5 versions.

Although not identified within the book, the author is Dave Giorgio. After I reviewed the book in my blog, Dave wrote the following in October, 2010:

"I'd like to respond to this, since I am mentioned in the article. There are valid points written here. I'd like to explain some things.

I think what had happened with that book is kind of like the story of the shoemaker who worked so hard on everyone else's shoes, that he looked down one day to see that his own shoes had holes in them.

The book was written around 2001. It was edited by Melanie Rigney, who is excellent. At that time, it was at least pretty good if not very.

However, I left the printed books side of things in 2005 and the book was not kept quite as current as it could have. There is still, even now, a lot of relevant content. But as pointed out, for example, ebook publishing is a lot more desirable today than it was back then.

The book wasn't managed, but rather, added to by staff over the years. So it's possible that some things were added without the same level of attention that the book had originally been written with.

However, the only feedback received was that people found it really helpful. So there was no call to action to scrutinize it. That's the truth.

That being said, Infinity Publishing underwent an ownership change earlier this year, and one of the improvements targeted was the publishing guide. A process had long ago been initiated that will yield an up-to-date and helpful guide whose purpose is, yes, to reflect well on Infinity Publishing, but to also serve up some valuable information in the process.

I have seen about a dozen proposed book covers, and they are all excellent. I am not sure which one will be chosen, but it will be very, very good.

The ownership change is what brought about the recent ebook offering and other really good things are coming from that as well.

Infinity Publishing is a small company with a lot of really dedicated staff. Taking care of authors is a huge undertaking because there are so many nuances to each person's book, their situation, publishing in general, etc.

I agree. It's been time for the book to be redone. It hasn't had the attention it deserved. But it's not because Infinity doesn't care. Just like the busy shoemaker who loses track of his own, the staff all work 60-hour weeks trying to provide the best, most responsive service that it can.

So while the focus had at one time been taken off the printed book they send out, I believe that the focus on authors has been the right thing for them to do.

With the new publishing guide that is forthcoming, the shoemaker will have finally repaired his own shoes."

Update: In late August, 2011, I received a copy of the new edition of the book. It has less information to help authors and is more of an advertisement for Infinity. Sadly, the pages are formatted with full justification but NO HYPHENS. Word spacing is ugly, and there are many "rivers." Bad typography is inexcusable in a promotional publication for a publishing company. A prospective customer who knows how books are supposed to look may pick another publisher.

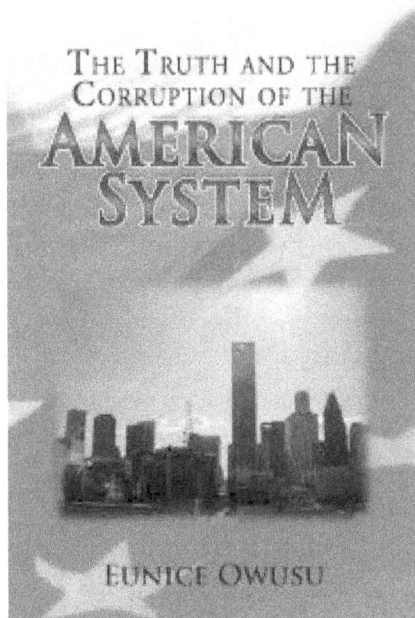

The Truth and the Corruption
of the American System
Eunice Owusu
Xlibris, 2009, 96 pages, $15.99 or $24.99

#7 **This potentially important book was ruined by its uncaring and mercenary publisher. It badly needs an editor.**

Traditional publishers like Random House make money by selling books to readers. Traditional publishers reject almost all of the books submitted to them.

Self-publishing companies make most of their money by selling services to writers. If a self-publishing company rejects a book, the company makes no money. That's why the self-publishing companies accept nearly every book submitted to them. Except for books that appear to be obscene or libelous, a self-publishing company will generally publish anything. There have been experiments where *intentionally horrible* manuscripts were published.

Lack of selectivity is the prime cause of self-publishing's bad reputation. Even though traditional publishers make many bad guesses—they frequently reject books which become successful with other publishers and accept books that quickly become failures—their selectivity and financial commitment do provide a powerful endorsement for the writers and books they choose to accept.

Self-publishing companies try to evoke an image of quality and service.

Xlibris says, "you can count on Xlibris' extensive experience to provide dependable, long-term, individualized support through the publishing process and in the years that follow." The company boasts about its "proficient team of publishing professionals" and says it has a "comprehensive range of publishing, editorial, add-on and marketing services."

Xlibris is one of several former competitors including iUniverse, Wordclay and Trafford which were absorbed by Author Solutions, Inc. "ASI" is also the private-label service provider for some traditional publishers such as Thomas Nelson. ASI says it produces "one of every 15 book titles published in the US every year."

At the 2010 Self-Publishing Book Expo, marketing director Joe Bayern told me that ASI's *best editors* work on Xlibris titles.

Xlibris says, "One of our founding principles, dating back to when we were newly incorporated and making books out of a basement office, is that authors should have control over their work. This principle still stands today as we help hundreds of authors every month publish their work in the manner and form that they envision," and "When you publish with Xlibris, you completely control the book design."

That's not necessarily a good thing. If an author has bad ideas for a book's design, or is simply a bad writer, crap gets published. The "proficient team" and "best editors" don't control the quality of what gets published with an Xlibris label.

One of the best examples (i.e., one of the *worst books*) that shows the failure of Xlibris is the awkwardly named, physically ugly, poorly written and unedited ***The Truth and the Corruption of the American System.*** The 95-page hardcover sells for (OMG!) $24.99. There are also paperback ($15.99) and e-book ($9.99) editions.

The author has some important things to say (more later), but the message is diluted and distorted by bad presentation and lack of help from Xlibris. The company wanted to collect money for the publishing package it sold her, but made no effort to improve the book.

Sales are probably infinitesimal. (Did *I* buy the only copy?) After more than two years, there is *not even one review* on either the Amazon or the Barnes & Noble website.

Author Eunice Owusu tells us on the back cover, and inside the book and on multiple websites: "I was born in Ghana and came to America about twenty-five years ago. I was married for twenty years and now separated with one child, who is seventeen years old. He lives with me in Houston, Texas. I attended Northern Virginia Community College and graduated in the year 2002 with Associate Degree in Legal Assisting. I transferred to George Mason University in Virginia, Texas Southern University in Texas, and now I am in my final year at the University of Houston in Texas, major in Political Science and eventually transfer to Law School."

- Does any of this provide a reason to buy a book about what's wrong with America?
- Do we care about Eunice's bad marriage?
- Do we care about her bad writing?
- Are we impressed by Northern Virginia Community College?
- Do we care about the age of the author's son?
- Do we know or care how old he is *now*, or that at one point he lived in Houston?
- Should we have to do research to determine if the author graduated from the University of Houston and went to law school?

Xlibris says it offers "seven comprehensive publishing packages, each with a unique combination of marketing, editorial and publishing services." It appears that unless an author pays $3,299 for the "premium package," the unique editorial service is *no* editorial service.

Five of the packages do not include editing, but the company says that **"Writing that is worth publishing is worth a careful edit. Your message deserves it, and so do your readers. It is what distinguishes a professional book from an amateur one."**

That's very true. Xlibris knows what's *right*, but lets its author customers do what's *wrong*.

Xlibris would rather sell a package for $649 with no editing and publish a crappy book than lose the sale because a writer won't pay $0.12 per word for editing. (The charge to copyedit the Owusu book would have been about $600.)

The book *badly* needs copyediting. Problems include lots of improper punctuation, sentence fragments, wrong tenses, wrong words, missing words, misspelling, missing possessives, improper uppercasing, inconsistent uppercasing, inconsistent time designations (e.g., "6:30" and "six-thirty" in successive sentences, "seven sixteen" and "7:20" in the same paragraph), repeated words ("do do" and "on on"), singular nouns that should be plurals, plural verbs that should be singular, sentences that should be two sentences, paragraphs that should be three paragraphs, unattributed quotations, numbers stuck in the middle of paragraphs for no discernible reason, unnecessary italics, and many more unforgivable errors.

There is lots of weird and crappy writing, such as:

- "The state Capitol is in Washington D.C. where Congress and Senates meet."
- "Something I did not understand about John McCain, when he was running for president, he run in favor of veterans."
- "Excuses are not accepted as there will also be an excuse."
- "I belief there are many homeless . . . ."
- "What can kind of normal person will eat and drink from trashes . . . ."
- "I make complain to . . . ."
- ". . . he was asked to do sports physical done."
- ". . . doctor run a series of tests."
- ". . . this was her respond."
- "I had to taken all my problems to bed. . . ."
- "It has to start from home, yes, and to schools."
- "Third ward in Houston don't even have head start."
- ". . . . here me out."
- ". . . . unplanned pregnancies that want to have an abortion."
- "Who will want to put their selve in . . . ."

Eunice came to America from Ghana as an adult. I know little about the schools in Ghana, but Ghana was a British colony until 1957 and the official language is *English*. Apparently, Eunice's English was good enough in her native country, but I am horrified to read what she writes now.

Another frightening example: ". . . they go on, on a wild goose chase which brings nothing but destruction to our country. This book also deomonstrate [*sic*] how we can keep kids off [*sic*] jail and minimize the high school drop off [*sic*] rate. How we can provide shelter for our return [*sic*] soldiers and civilian homeless."

The book contains a lot of criticism of American schools. Eunice attended at least four colleges in the United States and intended to become a lawyer.

Didn't *any* of her instructors or professors notice her bad writing? How did she get her diplomas?

The promotional work provided by Xlibris is confusing, inadequate and incompetent. Somehow, this book of social and political commentary is classified as "JUVENILE FICTION/Social Issues/Emotions & Feelings" and the reading level is said to be "Ages 9-12."

Xlibris says, "you will be treated with professionalism and courtesy and provided with all the self-publishing help you need." That's simply not true. Eunice Owusu was *not* treated with professionalism, and Xlibris did *not* provide all of the help she needed.

The design and production work provided by Xlibris is substandard. Page margins are much too small. It's silly to have the author's biography in two places. The author's photo on the back cover has awful composition and lighting. The text on the back cover is nearly illegible. There is no title on the spine. (The spine is small, but has room for a title.)

The copyright page includes this absurd notice: "This is a work of fiction. Names, characters, places and incidents are the product of the author's imagination or are used fictitiously, and any resemblance to any actual person, living or dead, events, or locales is entirely coincidental."

Oh, come on!

Is the following sentence fiction? "A fixed interest loan is a loan where the interest rate doesn't fluctuate during the fixed rate period of the loan."

Did the author invent Houston or the State Department? Is it a mere coincidence that the author conceived of a presidential candidate named John McCain?

Didn't anyone at Xlibris read—or even skim—this book?

As an immigrant and a single mother, Eunice Owusu has a special perspective. She has seen aspects of America that many Americans don't know—or care—about. Her outrage at shortcomings and inequalities is justified. She has important things to say. She deserves to be heard. She has experience and passion and provides needed recommendations. She may be a dynamic public speaker, but she is *not ready* to write a book by herself. Maybe she needed a ghostwriter or a co-author. At a minimum, she needed editing, but she got *none* from Xlibris.

That is a tragedy; and Xlibris and its parent, Bertram Capital Management, should be embarrassed by the terrible book they published for Eunice Owusu.

Self-publishing companies have to stop behaving like prostitutes who provide service to anyone who can pay the price.

Self-publishing companies need to develop some pride, and to grow some balls. They need to be able to say, "I'm sorry, but your manuscript is just not good enough to be published unless it gets professional editing." (Some manuscripts are beyond help.)

There is no solution if Xlibris and AuthorHouse reject books, and the penurious or egomaniacal author then goes to Outskirts Press or Lulu and they don't enforce editorial standards.

Until and unless ALL of the self-publishing companies develop and insist on high standards, readers will be buried in crap and writers' dreams will never come true.

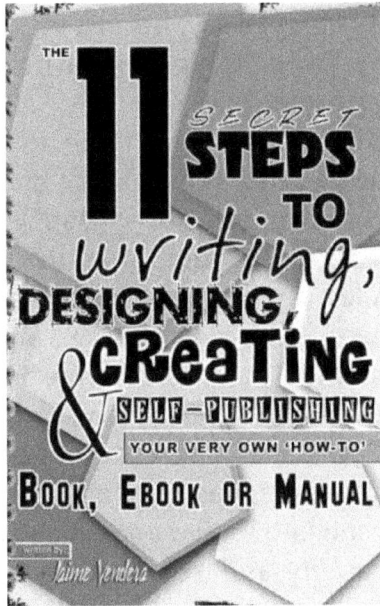

11 Secret Steps to Writing, Designing, Creating &
Self-Publishing Your Very Own 'How-To' Book,
Ebook or Manual
Jaime Vendera
Vendera Publishing, 2008, 136 pages, $19.95

#8

This author tried to do the right thing—but it turned out wrong. I don't like the book, but I do like the author. He knew not to do everything himself, but his helpers need help.

Jaime Vendera, author of *11 Secret Steps to Writing . . .*, has some important things to say, but his message is hurt by bad presentation. He knew enough to get help, but he got help from the wrong people.

Lots of self-published authors write books that try to teach other people how to self-publish. Some books—such as those written by Joel Friedlander, Christy Pinheiro, Morris Rosenthal, Aaron Shepard (and me, of course)—are quite good. Some are OK. A few are very poorly written. Several are physically unattractive. Some are like self-publishing parodies, showing what should *not* be done. Some books are dangerous because of the misinformation and bad advice they provide.

I slammed Theresa A. Moore, author of *Principles of Self-Publishing*, because she was extremely careless, knows less than she thinks she knows, has an unjustified high opinion of her own editing ability, and frequently ignores her own advice. Her book is ugly, inaccurate and sometimes poorly written. Theresa did the design and editing herself—and it shows.

I have mixed feelings about Jaime's book.

As with Theresa's book, there are a great many things wrong with this book, but the author *tried* to do things right, and was pleasantly responsive to my emailed questions and suggestions.

Unlike many self-pubbers, including Theresa, Jaime knew enough to hire a professional cover designer, editor and interior formatter. But they simply did lousy work and Jaime didn't realize it.

Jaime talks a lot about the members of his "team" and recommends them to other authors. Based on the evidence provided in the book, other authors should stay far away from this team.

If this book is an audition for Jaime's team members, they failed the audition. If this book is a crime scene, Jaime Vendera seems to be largely the victim of others, rather than a lone perpetrator like Theresa A. Moore.

- Editor/interior designer Amy Chesbro (whom Jaime calls "an amazing woman") did a TERRIBLE job.
- Jaime wrote about a "Forward" but Amy did not eliminate the unnecessary uppercase, or change the word to the proper "foreword." A book editor should know what a foreword is.
- The book lists one possible book size as 5-1/2 × 8.5"—using both a fraction and a decimal for "one half" within the same designation. A professional book editor should have caught this.
- The book says, "every singer with which I've worked." A book editor should have changed "which" to "whom."
- The book says, "books that I layout are." A book editor should have changed the noun "layout" into the verb phrase "lay out."
- The book uses curly typographers' quote marks to indicate inches instead of the proper straight *double primes*. A book editor should have known this.
- The book repeatedly refers to "Lightning Source Printing." That's not the name of the company, and both the writer and editor should have known this.
- The book has "self-publishing" (with hyphen) and "self publishing" (no hyphen), in successive lines. An editor should have caught this.
- "Acknowledgements" is spelled British-style. Here in the USA, there is no "e" after the "g."
- "Web site" and "website" are on the same page.
- There are silly typos, such as "then" for "ten" and "needles" for "needless." All books have typos, but these should have been easy to spot and fix. Ironically, Jaime quotes his website designer Molly Burnside: "Typos are

unavoidable, but easily fixed. Always have 10+ people check your site for silly mistakes. Silly mistakes make you look as if you don't pay attention to details, and in today's society, every detail translates into dollars and cents, so make sure you are focused on every period, quotation, and word!"

- "Ingram Advanced Catalog" should be "Ingram Advance Catalog."
- Jaime says, "Make sure to have your book layout completed right." He didn't do that. He also says that Amy Chesbro is "pretty well fitted in the interior design department." Jaime is not a good judge. Strangely, Daniel Middleton is also identified as the interior designer, so maybe he and Amy collaborated on the disasters.
- The book quotes Daniel on the perils of self-publishing: "substandard interior designs and garish covers, with typos, grammatical errors and phrasing issues." This book is a perfect example of what Daniel warns about. It shows a lack of knowledge and experience, and bad artistry.
- There are inconsistent spellings, misspellings, improper punctuation and even a fundamental lack of knowledge of the parts of a book.
- Per Jaime's preference, there are no hyphens, which lead to ugly word spacing, rivers, orphans and wasted paper. It's OK to skip hyphens in a website or e-book where the settings of the viewing device cause text to reflow—but lack of hyphens make a printed book ugly.
- Ironically, this is the fifth ugly non-hyphenated book I've read that tries to instruct authors how to self-publish. What's the problem with hyphens, folks?
- The footer on each page (i.e., both verso and recto in each spread) shows an abbreviated version of the title. It's unnecessary—and silly—to have it on both pages.

- Paragraphs are separated by empty lines, and are not indented. That's OK for a web page, but not for a book.
- The body text is sans serif. That's OK for a web page, but not for a book.
- The chapter titles and subheads appear to be in the same sans serif type face. The only variation is the word "TIP," probably in Courier, in the text boxes. The normal format for an American book is to use a serif face for body copy and sans serif for chapter titles and subheads—or at least a different serif face. Using one face for 99.9% of the words in a book is BORING.
- The index is strange. It was done by a PC with minimal human intervention, and the human who did intervene made some bad decisions. There are over 100 useless listings for the word "book," but just one each for "Amazon" and "Lightning Source," (which are both on *many* pages in the book), and none for "acknowledgment." "ISBN" is strangely set in bold face, but no other entry is treated that way. Some terms, such as "voice recorder" and "Mindset"—that nobody would look for—are indexed.
- The book has useful tips presented in text boxes. Unfortunately, the text boxes extend beyond the normal margins and some disappear into the binding.
- OK, I have a *compliment:* Despite abundant errors in interior formatting, the pages look infinitely better than Theresa's pages. Margins all around are ample, which make the pages both more attractive and easier to read.
- Back to the complaints: The clumsy title is hard to read.
- On the front cover, the author's name is in a barely legible script font that looks like a scribble.
- The cover says, "written by . . . ." That's amateurish.
- The spine of the book is covered with the image of a

spiral notebook's coil binding. Upon close inspection, I found that the book's TWENTY-WORD title is buried in the graphic in fly-turd-size type.

- Upon even closer inspection, I found that the title was printed *upside down*. A professional book designer should have caught this.

- When I used a magnifying glass (I'm not kidding), I found the author's name. Unlike the title, it was right-side-up. A tip: if text on the spine (or anywhere else) is too small to read without mechanical enhancement, it's TOO DAMNED SMALL.

- The text on the back cover is in slightly-larger-than-fly-turd-size type. However, the mini-words are made even more difficult to read because of the multicolored background. The words use small caps instead of lower-case letters. That's OK for a title or a headline, but not for text.

- The back cover says the book has "solid advice" and "no filler." Some advice is definitely not solid, and there is lots of filler.

- Jaime is very easily impressed. He notes that Lightning Source provides "your own username/password" for ordering books. So what!

- He says that a book can be set up with Lightning for a little over $100, but another company charged over $500. There's a very good chance that the $500 included interior formatting, cover design and other services. It's not a fair comparison.

- Jaime urges self-pubbers to open accounts with PayPal to accept credit cards for book purchases. That's a bad idea for two reasons. Some people don't like to use Paypal, and self-pubbers are much better off letting booksellers like Amazon handle sales, shipping and payments. Why should a writer have to operate a warehouse and shipping department? Amazon.com probably gets a million times the traffic of Jaime's website. I bought Jaime's book on Amazon—not from his site.

- Jaime had a very bad experience using Adobe Acrobat to produce a PDF file of a book. He warns, "if you convert and submit yourself, I can almost guarantee you that the file will be rejected." Jaime says that PDF conversion is an "art-form" and he even credits Brandy Cross for doing his PDF. Jaime says that both of his recommended experts "know how to . . . embed all fonts." Actually, it takes just a few seconds and a few mouse clicks to make a PDF with Adobe Acrobat. If I want fonts embedded, I merely uncheck a box to "rely on system fonts only." That requires no artistry or expertise.
- Jaime is similarly timid about resizing graphic images himself, and pays others to do it for him. (It's really not a big deal for anyone who owns a mouse.) Jaime warns that large photographs can "turn a 500kB book into a 3MB book." The file size for a book is a non-issue unless it's being stored on Jurassic-era floppy disks or uploaded with a Cro Magnon's modem. One of my recent book's file size as a Word doc is about 35MB, but the final PDF size is less than 6MB. It can be uploaded to my printer's website in less than a minute. There's no need to make the file size smaller.
- Jaime suggests offering a discount larger than the normal 20% most self-pubbers provide because "Amazon might quit promoting your book in the 'customers who bought this item also bought . . .' section." The 20% discount has not affected Amazon's promotion of my books—or many other books.
- The book has self-serving promotions for Jaime's own publishing company and website registration company.
- Jaime wastes a lot of space extolling the dubious virtues

of the people involved in producing the book.

- It's a thin book with just 134 pages of text, but it's padded with five pages copied from the Lightning Source website. There are three blank pages in the back that could have contained text—perhaps a larger index.
- In his section on book pricing, Jaime recommends "viewing prices and page counts of books similar to yours." If Jaime followed his own advice, his book would be bigger and less expensive.
- The title is "11 Secret Steps . . ." but I could not find *any* secrets. Steps such as deciding if illustrations are needed, having a cover on the book and converting a word processing file into a PDF are not secrets equal to the Manhattan Project or the Coke formula.
- Jaime cautions against a do-it-yourself website because it fried his brain. It's very easy to do a website. I've done it over 100 times, with no special training. I'm an amateur, but a few of my sites have won awards, and they've sold millions of dollars worth of products.
- Jaime says, "Many authors add an Acknowledgements section at the very end of the book." In the United States, there is no "e" before the final syllable in "acknowledgment," and every acknowledgment page I've seen is part of the *front* matter.
- In a tip about quoting other authors, Jaime recommends using "MLA or APA style to let people know the works you drew from." He does not explain what MLA and APA are. I've heard of a Modern Language Association but don't know if that's the MLA Jaime means, and I don't know what the APA is. Anglican Province of America? American Psychiatric Association? American Pregnancy Association? American Poultry Association? Automatic Pizza Apparatus?
- Jaime writes in a friendly, conversational style, but

sometimes it seems juvenile, unprofessional and inappropriate. He wrote, "Hello fellow authors; my name is Jaime Vendera" and "Now go make me proud . . . ."

So, what's *good* about the book?

- Jaime provides a detailed look at his bad experience with a company that provided a (failed) campaign to make one of his books an Amazon bestseller for $2,600. I knew these services were bad, but Jaime offers a valuable personal insight.
- He provides good advice on book promotion, particularly getting reviews.
- Jaime suggests producing an 8.5 × 11-inch instructional manual as an additional book format. I may try that.
- His anecdotes about finding suppliers and choosing a URL are interesting.

Jaime claims to be an "internationally known vocal phenom" who has cracked a glass with his voice. He self-pubbed a few books about vocal training and self-improvement, and now thinks he knows enough about publishing to teach others. Unfortunately, he has more to learn before he is ready to teach.

It's sad that this author—who has some important information and valid insights to present—chose helpers who produced an ugly and error-filled book.

Also, at $19.95 for just 134 pages, this book is grossly overpriced compared to the competition. (Commercial break: My book, *Get the Most out of a Self-Publishing Company: Make a better deal. Make a better book*, has 366 pages and a $17.95 cover price.)

Jaime wrote, "Be ready for a possible retaliation from the other author if you post a bad review." Actually, I don't think Jaime will beat me up or hire a hit man when he reads this. I know Jaime knows I want him to succeed. Actually, I want all writers to succeed—however they define success.

Although I have self-pubbed many books, I am still an amateur. I never went to "book publishing school" or sat next to a master book designer. All of my knowledge comes from research, observation, experimentation and questioning. Anyone could have learned what I've learned and could make books as good as mine, or even much better than mine. I honestly think that any self-pubber can and should make at least semi-pro-quality books, and most of the mistakes I criticize could have been easily avoided.

- Every self-pubbed book should be a learning experience. Jaime meant well, and I believe he'll learn from his mistakes and produce better books in the future.
- Unfortunately, I strongly doubt that Theresa A. Moore, Helen Gallagher or David Rising will do any better with future books. Their main problem is not ability, but attitude.
- They don't know enough to know that they don't know enough. That's a mix of ignorance and ego that affects do-it-yourselfers in every field. Homemade airplanes can crash and kill.

While Jaime's book happens to be about self-publishing, it reveals the potential perils for a writer dealing with any how-to topic, whether it's skiing, cooking or carpentry. Just because you've been successful at something, don't assume you know enough to teach others how to do it. And, check out the competition so you'll know if you can offer something new or better or less expensive—or all three. If you can't, you probably shouldn't publish.

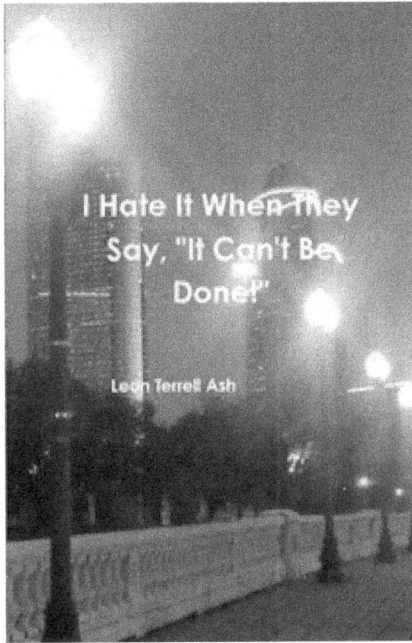

I Hate it When They Say "It Can't Be Done!"
Leon Terrell Ash
Lulu, 2011, 58 pages, $20

#9 **This undersized, overpriced and dreadful book should be euthanized. The author is an ignorant egomaniac who should not be permitted to touch a keyboard.**

On SPANnet (an authors' online group), newbie Leon Terrell Ash confessed to making a stupid and expensive mistake (apparently paying over $2,000 to print and send 300 copies of his book to "bookstores, and agents and famous people.") He wrote, "I have excepted the fact that this was a major insult to intelligence."

I responded, ". . . the proper word is 'accepted'— not 'excepted.' If your book has errors like this one, marketing won't help it."

Leon then said, "the books dont have errors. Perfect is how I would describe the writing."

Even this brief defense has a missing apostrophe in "don't" and the second sentence is strangely Yoda-ish.

Since I am cynical enough to know that no book is perfect—not even the "Good Book"—I had to take a look.

I visited the author's website and was not really surprised to find errors mixed with egomania and *really bad writing*.

Leon wrote, "I realized that I had created a masterpiece and did not want to share the credits with a publishing company that did not help in any type manner. I authored, edited, typeset and did the graph [sic] design. Terrell Ash Publishing seeks excellence in all avenues we pursue that deal with the advancement. Progress, a true word that I promote. This company believes that in order to get to your desired successes a person must learn to give away freely what God has given them."

The site shows the covers of two books the author proudly designed. They are both *ugly and amateurish*.

One book is a 58-page paperback selling for $20! How many did he sell? Probably somewhere between zero and none. Is he out of his mind? The e-book version is priced at $10. That confirms it. He *is* out of his mind.

What happened to "give away freely?"

Here's the horrid description of this horrid book: "The Goal of this autobiography was to inspire and help reinvigorate the belief people once had in themselves. It is an autobiographical guide to living a better life." Do we really need to be told it's an autobiography in two consecutive sentences?

Surprisingly, there was no online preview for the e-book. Is Leon hiding something?

Not surprisingly, I found just one review: "Excellent book! Everyone should have a copy." *The idiot author wrote the review!* He was not even smart enough to use a fake name.

I decided to invest (i.e., throw away) ten bucks. I may be the only one who ever buys this book, and I paid ten bucks for 58 pages. Oops—there are only about 40 pages of text. The book is grotesquely padded, perhaps in a futile effort to hide how little purchasers receive for their money.

The book is ugly and mostly uninteresting and it includes some terrible errors that new self-publishers make—and at least one I'd *never seen before*.

- The text is double-spaced, flush left, very-ragged right. It has no hyphens, but it does have orphans.
- Type that is supposed to be centered is off-center.
- Some punctuation is ancient typewriter-style, not proper curlies.
- The typeface is, of course, Times New Roman (a major faux pas).
- No sans serif type is used anywhere, not even in chapter names or subheads.
- Words that should be capitalized, are not—and vice-versa.
- Some words, like "grandmother," appear with and without initial caps.
- Blank pages have numbers.
- So do pages with nothing but section names.

- There are many grammatical errors which would not be tolerated in fourth grade.
- Some chapters start on the tops of pages. Some start half-way down.
- One paragraph fills a page and a half.
- There are extra spaces between many sentences—but not all sentences.
- Some sentences just don't make sense. Neither do the author's poems (e.g., "When Ten Commandments are given from you").
- Leon wrote "breathe" instead of "breath."
- **The book makes a stupendously stupid error which I heard of, but never saw before.** I thought this foul-up exists only in theory, but Leon did it *for real*. Pathetically ignorant, he put the odd-numbered folios on verso pages (i.e., odd page numbers on left-hand pages).

This author who says he seeks excellence did not want to risk the chance of his book being messed up by an editor—so he messed it up himself.

The book needs editing—or maybe euthanasia.

In a chapter about money, Leon says, "I have purchased enough books on money that I no longer have any money. Maybe I should ask the authors of those money books how to get the money back that I wasted on their book."

I understand Leon's disappointment. I've purchased a great many books, but have never asked for a refund. I *will* ask for a refund on this one.

Leon is a nurse. In a promo for his book about nursing, he spells "spell bound" as two words. He is definitely guilty of literary malpractice. If you are his patient, be sure to have someone else verify the drugs he plans to give you. He is ignorant and sloppy. That's a dangerous combination.

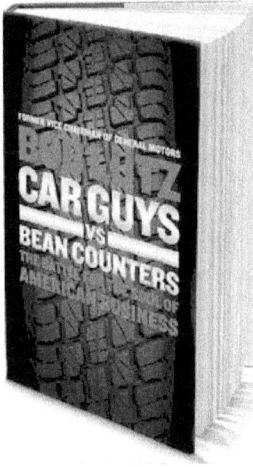

:ally with the United States, was
>ro-Western stability in the area.
it was determined that the best
for the United States to tacitly
yen to a <u>le vel</u> below that justi-
ages, balance of payments, and
nistrations of both parties, while
s of protest against "blatant cur-
panese, did precisely nothing to

#10 Dishonorable Mention: a silly error in a "professional" book

Do-it-yourself publishers are not the only ones who produce defective books. *Car Guys vs. Bean Counters* was published by Portfolio, an "imprint" of the Penguin Book Group. Penguin is one of the largest book publishers in the world and started in 1935. A publisher with vast size and long experience should know what it's doing—but doesn't always do the right thing.

The Penguin Riverside imprint published a phony auto-biography, *Love and Consequences.* Before the hoax was revealed and the book was recalled, it received an excellent review in the *New York Times*

Bob Lutz's *Car Guys* book exhibits a much smaller sin—a stupid typesetting error that should have been noticed by one of Penguin's experts before printing. Otherwise, it's mostly a good book.

Appendix

Assorted useful info

Here's a hyphen: ▪

Here's a minus sign: ▬

Here's a figure dash: ▬

Here's an en dash: ▬

Here's an em dash: ▬▬

Besides hyphenating, use the hyphen for "minus," (unless you are such a stickler that you want to use the REAL minus sign) and as part of a phone number or other numerical sequence if a *figure dash* is unavailable. (YES, I know that the figure dash looks like the en dash. There is a theoretical difference that's understood by a few guys on top of a mountain in Nepal, or maybe in a Burger King in Palo Alto.)

Use the en dash for ranges, such as June–August, 5:00–7:00 p.m., Ages 3–6.

Use the en dash to show contrasts or relationships: The Yankees beat the Mets, 24–6.

Use a pair of em dashes for a parenthetical remark—like this—when you want something more dramatic than parentheses or commas will provide.

An em dash can be used at the end of an interrupted quotation: Then Bill said to the robber, "I sure hope you're not going to—"

The em dash can also function as a "soft colon" in informal writing: This is the deal— if you won't wash the dishes, I won't cook. (In a case like this, I think a single dash should be attached to the preceding word with no added space, but there should be a space *after* the dash, as with a colon.)

Biggest business blunders of self-publishing authors

Paying too much for a self-publishing package (If you pay $5,000 or $50,000 it will be nearly impossible to earn back your cost of publishing.)

Paying too little for a self-publishing package (If you pay under $400, you will probably get terrible books.)

Not paying for professional editing

Not budgeting for promoting your book

Allowing a big "discount" for bricks-and-mortar booksellers which probably won't stock your book anyway, and giving up the additional profit you could get from online sales

Assuming that your publisher or printer will do a good job of promoting your books

Assuming that your book will be reviewed without trying to get it reviewed

Not having a website and blog

Assuming that your publishing company's website will sell lots of books for you.

Pricing your book too high

Pricing your book too low

Producing your book in only one format: you should have one or two print formats, plus one or three e-book formats.

Waiting until the book is printed to start marketing

Not having an understandable title

Not having a subtitle that can help sell the book

Writing & editing tips

Sometimes it can be very tough to type the first word. "Writer's block" affects most people who have to write—professionals as well as school kids. It can be caused by a lack of creative inspiration, by fear of writing the wrong thing, by hatred of the subject matter, by depression or even by an uncomfortable chair or a keyboard at the wrong height. The blockage can last for minutes, hours, days or decades.

For a student, writer's block might mean an "F" on a term paper. For a professional writer, the effects can be much worse. I was fired from my first job as assistant editor of a magazine when I had a two-week dry spell. Since I don't want that to happen to you, I'm glad to offer a simple and proven trick that should help you avoid either flunking or firing.

The opening word or phrase is undeniably important, but the importance can cause impotence. Fear of writing the wrong words can be like sexual performance anxiety or stage fright. The longer you stare at a blank sheet of paper or PC monitor, the more anxiety-inducing writing will become.

The need (or desire) to create something monumental like "It was the best of times, it was the worst of times," or "In the beginning, God created the heavens and the earth," or even "It was a dark and stormy night" can immobilize a writer.

Here's a simple cure for writer's block: if you can't write the first word or first sentence, JUST SKIP IT. Start farther down where you're more comfortable, and just *write*. Often, a book's beginning is an introduction. Once you've finished writing everything else, it will be much easier to write the introduction because you'll know what you're introducing.

◆It's hard to make a good index. Even good books have bad indexes. If you are sure you need to have an index, be prepared to invest a lot of time in it (when you might rather be doing

something else) or maybe invest a lot of money to have someone else do it.

◆At the end of each day or after a major revision, save your
book with a new file name. I like to use number sequences like
software: 1.01, 1.02, etc.

◆Save your book onto your PC's hard drive *and* also
onto portable media such as a USB thumb drive.
Keep backup files outside of your primary
workplace. Thumb drives are very inexpensive. You can afford to stash backups in *two*
places. Or three. You can also store files on
the "cloud." **www.Mediafire.com** is good, and free.

◆You can often spot errors if you *look* at pages, but don't actually read what you are seeing.

◆Don't hyphenate words in chapter titles. Move the word
down to the next line.

◆Make sure your PC has a functioning
back-up battery (*Uninterruptable Power
Supply*, or *UPS*.) I've had good luck with
UPSes from Minuteman, Tripp Lite, APC
and Belkin.

◆Watch out for unintentional changes. Microsoft Word can be
independent, and nutso. It's not uncommon for line spacing to
change or type to be dark gray instead of real black. It's easier
to spot aberrations if you magnify the page up to 150 or 200%
of normal size. The magnification also makes it easy to spot
errors which were imported when you copied and pasted from
other sources, especially straight quote marks and apostrophes
that were supposed to have been changed to curlies. Word

loves to put in horizontal lines (*rules*) where they don't belong and it can be extremely difficult to remove them.

♦Although Word can make numbered lists automatically, the lists may be inconsistent and unstable. It's sometimes better to insert numbers manually from the Symbol section, like ③.

♦Many people have trouble with "less" and "fewer." "Fewer" applies to things that are counted (e.g., apples). "Less" applies to things that are measured (e.g., apple sauce), or to concepts (e.g., freedom). You can have less wine, but fewer bottles and fewer drinks. You can have less time to travel, but fewer days for your trip. The express checkout lanes in supermarkets should be for buying *10 Items or Fewer*, not *10 Items or Less*.

♦ (From Emma Ruff, English teacher in my sophomore year in high school): "You **lie** sometimes or someplace, but you **lay** something or someone." I've remembered that since 1961.

♦Traditionally, *who* is used for people, and *that* is used for non-humans. Dog owners, cat owners and the Associated Press recognize that a pet (probably above the level of fish) can be part of the family. Dogs, cats, and maybe even mice or turtles, get better treatment than inanimate objects. For an unknown animal, say, "Firemen rescued a cat *that* was stuck in a tree." If the animal has a known name, use *who*, plus *his/him/her/hers*. "Firemen rescued Fluffy, *who* was stuck in a tree."

♦"Unique" means one of a kind. It's an absolute—it can't be modified. All unique things are equally unique. Nothing can be "more unique" or "less unique" than any other thing. "Most unique" and "very unique" reveal ignorance about the English language. "Most unusual" and "very unusual" are OK, but never put a modifier before "unique."

◆ Put your book away for a few weeks or—even better—a few months. When you return to it, you will discover errors you missed before and will probably have gained new insights during your absence. You'll likely realize that words and chapters that once seemed brilliant now seem insipid, silly, immature, superfluous, inadequate, out-of-date or otherwise inappropriate. However, you will probably have thought of new bits of brilliance which you can now insert to elevate the level of contemporary literature.

◆ No matter how many times you read and reread, you will find mistakes in anything you've written. It's best to find them before the book is printed.

A while ago, just minutes before I had planned to send a book to the printer, I decided to check my table of contents. I had a feeling that, as I changed the length of some chapters, a page number might have changed. I actually found three wrong pages, and two chapters were missing from the table of contents. Don't let it happen to you.

◆ The combination of changing paragraph spacing, changing type size and eliminating or substituting words gives authors who format their own books a lot more control compared to being subject to the whims of other editors and typographers.

◆ I once decided to change a real name to a fake name in a book I was writing, to avoid embarrassing someone who might not want to be written about. I used Word's **Find and Replace** feature, which quickly made about a dozen substitutions.

But when I read through the chapter I was surprised to find a few instances of the old name which had escaped the **Find** function. ➔ It's important to do a manual verification, because Word might not notice hyphenated words or words with apostrophes or in their plural form as targets for replacement. Don't risk a lawsuit by leaving in a wrong name or word.

♦After days, weeks or years of staring at pages, it's easy to miss major goofs and little gremlins. Important work deserves a professional editor, or maybe even two.

But before it goes to the pros, let anyone who happens to be willing and handy read it—maybe even out loud—and see if he stumbles or notices anything weird that you didn't pick up.

You should listen closely, too. When words are verbalized, you absorb them much more slowly than when you scan a page with your eyes; and you're much more likely to notice errors, or awkwardness such as repetition of words or inappropriate alliterations. Fortunately for you, it's human nature to want to find fault, so there's a good chance that even an inexperienced, unofficial and untrained editor will spot some mistakes.

A book or magazine article that will sit around for a long time with your name on it deserves special care. For something with a tight deadline or that's less important—such as a blog or a website item which you can easily change—you can skip the professional editing and use a convenient unpaid amateur.

I write several blogs. I start around 3:30 in the morning. My wife would be *really* pissed off if I woke her up to read.

Even during normal business hours she's often pissed off when she reads what I've written, so I just have to trust my own editing ability (for blogs, not for books).

♦An ellipsis (plural is "ellipses") is a series of three dots which can have several purposes, be governed by several standards, and appear in several forms. I use three dots with no spacing (...) to indicate a pause, or a trailing-off into another phrase. I use three dots with spaces to indicate an omission. If the omission is at the end of a sentence, I use four, like . . . .

♦There are several standards for printing numbers (*figures*) in a book. One calls for spelling out one through nine, another says you should spell out numbers through ten. In "serious" literary books you may even see "ninety-three" or "four thousand." Select a system and *stick to it*. One book in the *For Dummies* series has "10" and "ten" in the same paragraph!

EXCEPTIONS:

1. Never start a sentence with a figure. Write: "Fourteen mayors are up for re-election," not "14 Mayors." You may need to rewrite to avoid awkwardness. You can say, "In 1982, the divorce rate rose to . . ." to avoid "Nineteen-Eighty-Two was the first year that the divorce rate reached . . . ."

2. Use the *same style* when numbers are nearby: "eight to twelve" or "8 to 12"—not "eight to 12."

3. Don't spell out numbers in addresses or prices, except for low numbers like "One Main Street" or "five bucks."

What does a self-publisher have to do?

1. Have at least one book idea.
2. Unless you are using a self-publishing company such as Xlibris or Outskirts Press and are willing to have its name on your books, pick a name for *your own* publishing enterprise. Think of several acceptable names and do some research so you can select one that's not already being used by another company in publishing or a related field.
3. Register the name in the local government office that registers names, often with the town clerk. You will get an "assumed name" certificate, "fictitious name" certificate, or a "DBA" (Doing Business As) certificate. You may be required to advertise the business name in a local newspaper.
4. Get whatever licenses or permits that your state or municipality requires.
5. Open a business checking account under the business name.
6. Get business cards.
7. Set up a website.
8. Set up a businesslike email address, not a free Gmail or Yahoo email account.
9. Write the first book.
10. Have the book copyedited and, if necessary, get more extensive editing.
11. Have the book read by several laypeople and, if the subject is in a specialized or technical field, by one or more experts on the subject.
12. Make the suggested changes.
13. Either gather the necessary photos, graphs and illustrations or have custom artwork made.
14. Either design the interior yourself or hire a pro to do it.
15. Either design the covers and spine yourself or hire a pro to do them. (You should probably hire a pro.)

16. Show several cover alternatives to people whose judgment you respect. Strive to stimulate thought and dialog—not merely "I like it," "I hate it," "OK," "wow" or "hmmm."
17. Put your manuscript into book-like format, using either Microsoft Word or a more sophisticated program.
18. Insert the artwork in the proper positions.
19. Read, read, read, and have others read, read, read—on the screen in multiple formats and on printed papers.
20. Establish an account with Lightning Source or CreateSpace so they will print and distribute your book—or use a self-publishing service if you want to do less work and are willing to have less control and make less money.
21. Promote, promote, promote. Let lots of potential readers know that your book exists and convince them to buy it. Promotion includes news releases, book reviews, comments on blogs and websites, email signatures, your own websites, distributing business cards, mailing out letters and post cards, signing autographs at bookstore sessions, and whatever else you can think of.

How long does it take?
How much does it cost?

These numbers are based on my experience and research. Your mileage may vary.

Time to write a book: between a week and a lifetime

Time to design a cover: a few hours to a few weeks

Time to copyedit: a few days to a few weeks

Time for major editing: a few weeks to a month

Time for ghostwriting: one to three months

Time for Lightning Source to process your files and ship out a proof: three business days

Time for CreateSpace to process your files and ship out a proof: two business days

Time for Lightning Source to print and ship a case of 20 books: two business days

Time to receive a proof after shipping by CreateSpace: one to five business days

Time to receive a proof after shipping by Lightning Source: one business day

Time for a book to be listed on Amazon.com after a proof is approved: a few minutes to a few days

Time to be listed on Barnes & Noble and other book websites after a proof is approved: two to five days

Time for a book to change from being *drop-shipped* by Lightning Source to being stocked by Amazon: a few days to a few weeks, or never

Time for a book to be discounted by Amazon: a few weeks to a few months, or never

Time until you get your first money from Lightning Source: three months. Then you get money monthly, if your book sells.

Number of printed proofs you'll correct before you decide your book is good enough to print: three to six

Cost of MS Office 2007: $110 - $500

Cost of MS Word 2007 alone: $85 - $230

Cost of Adobe Acrobat 9 and Distiller: $90 - $600

Cost for Lightning Source to print one 300-page 6✕9-inch book: $5.40

Cost for Lightning Source to print 50 more at the same time: deduct 5% (there are larger discounts for larger quantities)

Cost to design a cover: $200 to $1,000 or more

Cost to copyedit: $200 to $500 or more

Cost for major editing: $500 to $1,000 or more

Cost for ghostwriting: $5,000 or more (maybe a lot more)

Cost to ship a 300-page book by Priority Mail: $4.95

Cost for Lightning Source to ship one 300-page book the least expensive way: $3.80

Cost for Lightning Source to ship one 300-page book with tracking: $5.52

More expensive shipping service options for Lightning Source to ship one 300-page book faster: $7.27 - $36.40

Minimum markup percentage ("discount") Amazon will work on: 20% (or 10% if they give a discount to readers).

Understanding print on demand (POD)

Book agents and publishers are generally risk-averse. They tend to support books that are similar to successful books and to support authors who have attracted a loyal following.

Despite the experience and caution, the experts are usually wrong. Most books fail. Most books don't sell in sufficient quantities to earn back advances. Most books go out of print within six months of publication, and existing inventory is then remaindered and sold on the buck-a-book tables.

Print on demand removes most of the risk from book publishing.

The term pretty much explains itself. With POD, potential reading material is stored as digital files in computers, not as slices of dead trees on a shelf. The files are printed out as books when there is demand for them. Physical books don't exist until a reader or publisher causes an order to reach the printing company. It costs more to print each book this way compared to conventional *offset* printing, but there are few or no unwanted books to be stored or disposed of. There is no danger of spending money to print books that will not be sold.

The common offset presses are generally used for print runs of hundreds or thousands of books. It was not economical to print just one or a few books at a time until the recent development of high-speed laser printers that print and bind hundreds of pages in a minute.

A book manuscript that is going to be offset-printed requires fairly complex preparation including the production of printing *plates*. Offset presses use ink that can be printed on a wide variety of paper types. Digital printers use *toner* that bonds to pages with heat and will adhere to fewer types of paper. Offset presses have the potential to produce the best books, but most people won't be able to tell the difference between offset and digital books.

Early POD books were inferior to offset-printed books, but quality has improved continuously and considerably. Today the best POD books look as good as offset books, with the possible exception of photograph reproduction—but it's good enough and getting better all the time.

Preparation for POD is much simpler than for offset, but per-book cost is higher; and there is little saving as the quantity increases.

With offset, preparation cost can be amortized over varying quantities of books, so the per-book cost goes down as quantity goes up.

If a writer self-publishes, she is in charge of the entire project from beginning to end, and she pays all costs. To make the printing affordable using offset, the writer usually must print at least a few hundred copies. She then is responsible for distributing, selling and promoting the book.

A 300-page paperback printed by offset could cost $1.84 each for 1,000 copies or $1.17 each for 10,000, or even less for 100,000. With POD, one copy could cost $5.40. There's usually a 5% discount for 50 or more and higher discounts for larger quantities.

POD can also be used for hardcover books. The additional cost is typically $4–$7 more than each paperback. The difference at retail can be $10 or more.

Because POD books generally cost more to produce than offset books, in order for them to have competitive retail prices, they generally do not offer the large markup (called a *discount* in the book biz) that bricks-and-mortar booksellers expect and demand.

Another factor limiting sales from physical stores is the lack of *returnability*—an archaic practice peculiar to the book industry and seldom encountered with other retail products.

There is nothing to stop an independent self-publisher from allowing returns, but costs and risks are high. Some self-publishing companies offer returnability for an extra fee, but that cost cuts into the author's profits, and bookstores generally don't want to stock those books anyway. Returnability is a major cost even for traditional publishers, and the industry will likely eliminate or minimize returns sometime in the future. This shift could make it easier to get bookstores to stock self-published books.

Publishing terminology

This is a selective list. I avoided common terms like "design" and tried to include the most useful terms. I included some obscure terms that may not be very useful, but are interesting or fun—like "fleuron," "dingbat," "kern," "OOP," "hickey," "lede," "pilcrow" and "virgule."
More at www.cmykgraphix.com/?Page=glossary

Acid-free paper: Paper made without chemicals that cause paper to deteriorate. It costs more and lasts longer. This book is made from acid-free paper. Inexpensive mass-market paperbacks are not expected to be around for long and generally don't use acid-free paper.

Advance Reader (or **Readers** or **Reader's** or **Reading** or **Review**) **Copy:** A book from a Not-Ready-For-Prime-Time, limited print run, distributed for book reviews and publicity, usually about three to six months before publication of the final version of the book. Also called an "**ARC**."

Air: Graphics industry slang for the white spaces where there is no text or illustration. "Harry, the margins on this page design are too small. It needs more air."

Appendix: A section at the end of a chapter, or, more commonly, in the back matter of a book, that contains additional material, such as statistical tables which would not conveniently fit in the main part of the book

Artwork (art): Visual material, such as drawings, pictures and photographs used to explain, clarify or decorate a book. Sometimes called a "**graphic element**" or a "**graphic**."

Author's Alteration (AA): A change made to a book after it was assumed to be ready for printing, at the request of the author. Publishers usually charge for AAs.

Back matter (end matter): Material, such as appendixes (or appendices), notes, references, author's biography, bibliography, glossary and index—placed after the chapters of a book.

Back-of-the-room sales: Book sales made at table, usually in the back of or just outside an auditorium, at an event such as a conference or convention where the author is speaking.

Binding: The process, such as stitching or gluing, used to attach the pages of a book to its cover.

Bleed: When a photograph or illustration bleeds, it extends beyond the normal edge of a page or cover. When the paper is trimmed, the picture extends to the actual edge of the book, with no white space surrounding it.

Blurb: A brief quote from a reader, often someone famous, which is used to promote a book. Blurbs are often printed on book covers or on the first page.

Bodoni Bold: Evil son of Hagar the Horrible—and a cool name for a typeface. I learned about it in print shop in eighth grade.

Body copy: The main section of a book, between the front matter and the back matter. In an ad, it's words below the headline.

Boldface: Letters, words, phrases or sentences printed in **heavier and darker print** for emphasis.

Book block: A digital file containing the entire book except for the covers.

Bookland: A fictitious country created to reserve an EAN (originally *European Article Number*) Country Code for books, regardless of their country of origin. Country codes for Bookland are 978 and 979. Bookland is located north of Lower Slobovia, south of Grand Fenwick, east of Chelm and west of Oz. It's not far from Atlantis.

Breaker head (subhead): A distinct-looking word or phrase that runs between paragraphs, usually to introduce a section. It's often in large, bold type.

Bricks-and-mortar retailer: A physical store, as opposed to an online business. Some companies, such as Barnes & Noble, are both. Some people use the singular "brick-and-mortar." Since buildings use multiple bricks, I use the plural form.

Bulk: The thickness of paper in pages-per-inch ("PPI"), or the thickness of a book without its cover.

Casewrap: A hardcover book binding without a dust jacket.

Cataloging in Publication (CIP): Detailed book data on the copyright page of a book, and used in library catalogs

Character set: The complete set of letters, punctuation, etc. in a particular font.

Chick lit: Not to be confused with Chiclets candy-coated gum, it's chick literature—the print equivalent of chick flicks. The books are often romantic and written for women in their 20s and 30s. There are sub-genres for teen, matron, Latina, Christian and Asian chicks.

Clip art: Drawings and photographs that have few or no restrictions on use. Years ago, the artwork was printed on sheets of glossy paper and literally "clipped" apart and pasted into page layouts. Today, most clip art is digital.

Coated paper (coated stock): Smooth paper with a coating of clay or other substances to reproduce photographs better than the uncoated paper in this book. When used in books, coated paper generally has a glossy surface. When used for printing photos, it can have glossy, matte or other finishes.

Column inch: Newspaper jargon for how much space is used for an article. A typical column is a bit less than two inches wide and contains about 30 words—so five column inches can contain about 150 words. The number of column inches used for an article is an indicator of its importance.

Compressed: An extremely narrow typeface, narrower than condensed. Compressed faces are often used in movie posters. This is Bodoni MT Poster compressed.

Condensed: A typeface that is narrower than normal, but wider than compressed. This is Bodoni MT Condensed.

Consignment: A business method common in book publishing that allows dealers to return unsold products to the manufacturers (i.e., the publishers).

Co-op (co-operative) advertising: A plan where two businesses share the cost of advertising. Typically, a manufacturer (which could be a publisher) pays a percentage (usually 50%) of the cost of advertising products made by the manufacturer and sold by a dealer. Generally there are restrictions on media selection and ad content and limits to the expenditure.

Copy: Words written for or appearing in a book, article, ad, etc.

Copyeditor (CE, copy editor): This is the editor who concentrates on form, rather than on content. She (usually not he) corrects grammar, spelling, punctuation and inconsistencies.

Copyright: The government-backed rights to copy, publish or modify a creative work, such as a book, photo or website.

Co-venture: A business entity where expenses and responsibilities are shared by several people or business.

Crop marks: Small lines on a page design or cover design to indicate where it will be trimmed after printing. Nothing important should be placed outside the crop marks.

Crowdfunding (crowdfinancing): A method of raising money for a project, such as book publishing, by appealing to large numbers of people for small donations. It's often done through social media such as blogging and Facebook. Sometimes donors make outright gifts to support a project they believe in. Sometimes, there is an expectation of repayment, perhaps with interest. Sometimes, the donors are listed as sponsors of the project.

Cut line: newspaper jargon for the caption under a photograph or illustration. Before they published photographs, newspapers used engravings, which were often called "cuts."

Developmental editor: An editor, usually employed by a large publisher, who deals with the overall organization of a book rather than the fine-tuning done by a copyeditor. A developmental editor may suggest changes in a book's sequence and deletion or addition of material, and may even write some additional material as a ghostwriter.

Dingbat: Printers' slang for small, icon-like drawings of hearts, snowflakes and other shapes and items (◈ ⌘ ♦ ✈ ✂) which can be used to dress up a document. Also, what Archie Bunker frequently called wife Edith on *All in the Family.*

Discount: A percentage taken off the retail price of a book that is retained by a distributor, wholesaler and retailer. Also, a reduction from list price which saves money for shoppers.

Display type: Type used for book titles, chapter titles, subheads, etc. that is larger than the type used for the text.

Distributor: A "middleman" company that buys books from a publisher and sells them to a retailer. Unlike a wholesaler, a distributor usually has a sales force that calls on booksellers. A wholesaler usually just fills orders.

Domain name: A web address, also known as a URL (Uniform Resource Locator).

DPI (Dots per Inch): A measurement that represents the resolution ("sharpness") of a printer or scanner.

DRM (Digital Rights Management): the modification of a digital file, such as a book, song or movie, to prevent it from being copied in violation of its copyright.

E-book (electronic book): A book formatted and distributed as a data file rather than printed on paper. Various e-book formats are used with dedicated "readers," cellphones and PCs.

Edition: A particular version of a particular book. First editions are sometimes valuable.

End matter: See "Back matter."

Endnote: See "Footnote."

Endorsement: See "Blurb."

E-tailer: An online retailer.

Figure: Typographers' jargon for a number or numeral.

Flack: A derogatory term for a public relations (PR) person.

Fleuron: A flower-like decoration used to enhance a book or to divide sections.

Flong: One of my favorite words! A flong was originally a dry, papier-mâché mold made from type text which could be curved to fit the cylinder of a rotary press. Later flongs were wet, and made of plastic or rubber.

Flush-left/ragged-right: An informal typographic design in which the lines of text are aligned against the left margin but "run wild" on the right, as opposed to "justified" type. Flush-left is nearly universal for websites and is widely used in advertisements and periodicals. It is less common in books. See "justified" and next entry.

Flush-right/ragged-left: The opposite of above. It's seldom used for long text, but may be a good choice for headlines and short sections of text that have to appear distinctive.

Folio: A page number. Also a leaflet, a page size, a typeface and various other meanings. A **drop folio** is a page number in the **footer** at the bottom of the page, like this page. A folio is also a feature in some luggage such as a "pilot's case." A **blind folio** is a page number that is counted, but not printed.

Font: A specific typeface (e.g., Verdana) in a specific style (e.g., **bold**) and a specific size (e.g., 11 points).

Footer: Words or numbers below the main text on a page

Footnote: A reference or explanatory detail printed at the bottom of a page. Footnotes can be hard to keep in the right place as a book evolves, so "endnotes" either at the end of a chapter or at the end of the book may be easier to handle. If there are lots of notes, I recommend putting them at the end of each chapter to avoid forcing readers to scan through many pages of notes at the end of a book.

Foreword: An introduction to a book, written by someone other than the author; part of the front matter.

Formatting: At least three meanings: ①the process of "laying out" text and illustrations to convert a manuscript into a finished book page design; ②modification of letters, numbers, or punctuation to make them **bold**, *italic*, etc.; ③conversion of one type of data file into another, such as a Word file into a PDF (Portable Document Format).

Frontispiece: Seldom found in modern books, it's an illustration, often an engraving, facing a book's title page.

Front matter: The information that goes on the pages between the front cover and the main text of a book. It usually includes a title page, a copyright page, a table of contents, a dedication and various introductions.

Fulfillment house: A company that provides some or all of the order-handling work for a publisher, such as warehousing, packing, shipping and record-keeping.

Galley proof (galley, galleys): Galley proofs get their name from hand-set type. Years ago, a typesetter would prepare a book page by arranging pieces of type into a metal tray called a *galley*. The galleys for a book would be used to print a small number of copies for editing and proofreading, and some would be provided to reviewers and booksellers. After the author and editors marked up the galleys, the typesetter would make corrections and books would be printed and shipped. Today, it's more common for publishers to provide reviewers with **ARC**s rather than galleys.

Genre: A book's general category, such as chick lit, crime, sci-fi, historical fiction, fantasy, how-to, porn, business.

Gerund: A part of speech frequently used, but seldom thought about after third grade. It's a noun made from a verb, like "thinking," "eating" and "writing."

Ghostwriter: A writer paid by a publisher or by another writer to write or co-write a book. Some ghostwriters are unnamed in the book. Some are listed: "with Peter J. Ghostly."

Graf: Journalists' timesaving slang for "paragraph."

Graphic (graphic element, graphic image): Something on a page other than text or space—such as a photo or chart.

Grayscale: A graphic image with no color—just black, white and shades of gray, possibly converted from color.

Gutter: The vertical white space centered between the blocks of text and illustrations on two facing pages. In DaBronx, it's pronounced "guttuh," and is a synonym for "roadway," as in "Don't play in the guttuh—you could get hit by a cah."

Halftone: A method to prepare a photograph or other graphic image for printing by converting it into thousands of little dots of various sizes. If the dots are small enough, the printed image appears to be continuous, like a real photograph.

Hand selling: A personal book recommendation in a store, convention, trade show, book fair, etc.

Hanging indent (hanging indentation): A page design technique in which the first line of a paragraph is flush left and the following lines are indented, as on this page.

Hardcover book: A book with a cover made of cloth, leather, foil or other flexible material glued to rigid cardboard. Hardcovers are more durable and may look better than paperbacks.

Header (page header, running head): Words or numbers above the main text on a page, often in a distinctive typeface. Headers often include book title, author's name, chapter name and/or number, page number.

Hickey (bull's eye, fish eye): A spot or imperfection on a printed paper caused by dirt.

Independent publisher (indie): A small publishing company that is not a subsidiary of a larger publishing or media company. It may be a self-publishing author who also publishes books for others.

Initial caps: A Typesetting Style Where The First Letter Of Each Word Is Capitalized (set in "uppercase").

International Standard Book Number (ISBN): A unique, 13-digit number that identifies a version of a book. Until 2007, ISBNs had ten digits.

ISPITA: Industrial Strength Pain In The Ass (much worse than a mere PITA), common in publishing.

Justified: A typography design in which lines of text reach all of the way to the left and right margins of a page or a column.The first and last lines of a paragraph may be shorter than the others.

Kern: That's the way some people born in Brooklyn pronounce "coin." In typography, "to kern" means to adjust the spacing between two adjacent letters. It can also mean to squish two letters together so they overlap to avoid awkward white spaces. **WA** is one common use of kerning, and the two letters fit together unusually well. A kern is also a part of one letter that reaches into another letter's personal space—like the curled "hood" on this **f**.

Keyword: An important word or phrase that is typed into an online search engine to find relevant web pages. Websites and blogs can be "optimized" for keyword searches.

Layout: The overall design of a page, book, magazine, ad, sign or other graphic project. A "rough layout" is a quick preliminary sketch of the design. The preferred verb form is "lay out."

LCCN: Library of Congress Control Number used to identify books. The LCCN is frequently printed on the copyright page of a book, and used by many libraries.

Leading: Extra space added between lines of type. It rhymes with "bedding," and gets its name from thin strips of lead that were inserted between lines of type when type was set by hand. With modern typesetting, a designer can specify, for example, 11 point type with 13 point leading. This means that two points of extra space would be added between lines.

Lede: The first sentence or two in a news story, with the most important information. It's pronounced "leed", but spelled "lede" to avoid confusion with another typographic term, "lead," which rhymes with "bread."

Letter Spacing: Changing the spacing between characters in a block of text, like a headline—in contrast to **kerning** which deals with the spacing around individual characters. NOTE: letter spacing sometimes is used to mean kerning.

Ligature: Several letters joined together to improve appearance and save a little space.

Compare **fi** and **ffl** ligatures to **fi** and **ffl**

Line art: A graphic image made of solid lines, usually against a white background, common in cartoons and charts in modern publishing. Before photography and halftone printing, line art was the standard format for printed illustrations.

Line editor: Often the same as a **copyeditor**, but sometimes a line editor will make modifications, not just corrections.

Literary agent: A person who tries to interest a publisher in an author's work, and who usually is involved in contract negotiation and sale of subsidiary rights. If a deal is made, the agent gets a percentage of the author's income. Sometimes, an author can make a deal with a publisher without an agent, but this is uncommon with larger publishers.

Manuscript: Text and graphic elements of a book prepared by the author and usually submitted to an agent, editor or publisher. It can be either on paper or in a digital file.

Mass-market paperback: A small, less-expensive version of a hardcover book which is usually printed after the hardcover version has been on sale for about a year. Often not as nice as a **trade paperback** because of rough paper, small margins and poor photographic reproduction.

Media kit: See press kit.

Media release: See press release.

News release: See press release.

Offset printing: The common method used for printing large quantities of books, magazines, newspapers and brochures. Ink is spread onto metal plates with etched images of the pages, then transferred to an intermediary surface such as a rubber "blanket," and finally applied to paper by pressing the paper against the intermediary surface.

Out of print (OOP): A book that is no longer being printed but may still be for sale. ***Alley Oop*** was a comic strip, created in 1932 by V. T. Hamlin. He wrote and drew the strip through four decades. The stories combined adventure, fantasy and humor, and were often satires of American suburban life like the later *Flintstones* cartoon series. Alley Oop, the strip's title character, wore fur shorts, lived in Moo and rode a dinosaur named Dinny. (Houghton Mifflin would've removed this. When you self-publish, you can print *whatever* you want.)

Overrun: An extra quantity of books printed beyond the requested quantity. Printers often print additional copies of a book to make up for possible defective copies. If the extra copies are not needed to make up the required total, the customer is usually required to pay for an overrun of up to 10%.

Over the transom: See "slush pile."

Page proofs: Printed typeset pages that look like the interior of a book, but without the covers. They may not be trimmed to the size of the final book pages.

Parchment: The skin of a sheep or goat prepared for use as a material for writing or printing. Paper can also be made to look like real parchment. It's often translucent.

Pay-per-click advertising (PPC): An advertising payment system in which the advertiser pays the operator of a website, particularly a search engine, every time someone clicks on an ad that could lead to another website and will perhaps buy something, support a cause, etc.

P-book: The opposite of an e-book, it's Printed on Paper.

PDF (Portable Document Format): A digital document file format, developed by Adobe Systems, which allows a document to be accurately reproduced on computers using different operating systems.

Perfect-bound: The binding method used for most paperback books, including this one. Pages are glued to the spine.

Permission: Agreement from a copyright holder to permit another person or entity to use copyrighted material.

Pied type: Back in the days when type was set by hand, if a careless or lazy typesetter did not sort out the pieces of type after a print job, but just dumped them, the type was "pied."

Pilcrow: Symbol indicating where a new paragraph should begin. "Pilcrow" should be used more often. Try putting it in sentences like "Wow! Steve sure is a dumb pilcrow."

PITA: Pain In The Ass (not limited to publishing).

Prepress: Preparation of a manuscript for printing. POD printing requires minimal prepress.

Press kit (media kit): A package of promotional material sent to writers and editors and intended to announce and gain publicity for a new book. There are now online press kits as well as paper-based kits.

Press release (news release, media release, publicity release, PR release): It's an announcement distributed to the news media with the hope of receiving publicity for a new book or other product, person or event.

Print On Demand (POD): Manufacturing books in small quantities—even one—as orders are received.

Print-ready: The digital data files (usually in PDF format) that have been checked and are ready to be printed.

Proofreading: Reading of typeset pages to find errors. Years ago, proofreaders would compare a typeset page against the author's final edited manuscript. With self-publishing, the author may produce the equivalent of typeset pages, so proofreading is an intense reading before printing, with no comparison to a previous generation of text.

Publication date: The official date on which a book is allowed to be sold. It is often fictional and arbitrary because many books are sold before their "pub date."

Publicist: Formerly call a "press agent," it's a person who tries to generate media coverage for a book or an author by contacting the media. The publicist may also produce and distribute publicity materials and assist an author with personal appearances and other promotional activities.

Remainders: Books that are discounted to low prices, often one dollar, because they are outdated, damaged, selling poorly or excess inventory. A book may be "remaindered."

Returns: Books sent back from a bookstore to a publisher for a refund or credit because they did not sell.

Royalty: Payment to an author after books are sold, usually a percentage of sales in the 5 to 50% range. There's often a sliding scale for which higher rates are paid when sales reach certain thresholds. The rate may be applied to either the cover price or a publisher's net receipts. Pay attention.

Rule: In typography, it's a line used for separation or decoration, such as this one: ━━━━━━━━━━━ Rules are not called "lines" except for a "hairline rule," which is ½-pt high.

Running head: see "Header."

Sans serif (gothic): A typeface style like **Arial**—simple, with no serifs or other decorative effects. Sans serif faces are commonly used for chapter names and subheads in books.

Self-publishing: A writer's becoming the publisher of her or his own books, or using a self-publishing company.

Sell-sheet: A one-page flier, describing and promoting a new book, aimed at booksellers, distributors and the media.

Serif: A thin line attached to the top or bottom of letters, or other decorative effects such as the "flag" attached to the top of the lowercase "h," which may make text easier to read. Serif faces are generally used in books, but not on websites.

Short discount: A smaller-than-usual discount from the cover price of a book, common with POD books sold online. A short discount is typically 20%, compared to the standard discount of 50% or more with traditional sellers.

Sic: Latin word for "thus." It's used to indicate that the preceding error or unusual wording or punctuation was in the source, and not copied incorrectly. The word should be italicized and within square brackets like this: [*sic*]. "Sic transit gloria mundi" has nothing to do with ailing trains or buses. Look it up.

Signature: A large sheet of paper, holding multiple book pages and printed on both sides. A signature is folded and cut to become a group of pages. Years ago, printers *signed* their names to indicate that pages were OK.

Slush pile: Unsolicited manuscripts received by an agent or a publisher and often piled up on a desk, a shelf or the floor, awaiting evaluation or disposal. These are also described as "**over the transom**" manuscripts. The phrase refers to the horizontal bar above a door and below a hinged window provided for ventilation in an office without air conditioning. Writers allegedly tossed their manuscripts over the transom of a publisher's office and hoped for the best.

Small caps: SMALL CAPITAL (UPPERCASE) LETTERS ABOUT THE SAME HEIGHT AS LOWERCASE LETTERS. They're good for abbreviations and acronyms like FBI, A.M. and RADAR.

Small press: A small publishing company that produces a relatively small number of titles each year, often in niche subjects or for specialized audiences.

Spine: The narrow section of a book that connects the front and back covers and shows the title and the author's name.

Stet: Latin for "let it stand"—an editor's or proofreader's indication to cancel a previous change.

Style book: A book, produced by a publishing authority such as the *Associated Press* or the *New York Times,* which dictates standards for spelling, punctuation, etc.

Style sheet: A set of rules assembled by an editor, designer, publisher or writer which dictates the standards for spelling, punctuation, listings, spacing, fonts, abbreviation, etc.

Subhead (sub-headline): See "breaker head"

Substrate: Material that is printed on, such as paper or cloth.

Subtitle: Words below the title of a book which explain or amplify the title. A title should "work" without its subtitle. Subtitles are important for online searching.

Subsidiary rights: Rights sold by a book publisher for reuse of a book's contents in other forms, such as magazine excerpts, movie scripts or books in other languages.

Subsidy publishing: An uncommon publishing arrangement in which the publisher and author share the cost of publishing.

Supported self-publishing: Yet another term for a system where an author pays to produce books.

Swash: An extra bit of decoration added to a printed letter, often an extended or exaggerated serif on the first letter in a paragraph.

Swoosh: the Nike symbol designed by student Carolyn Davidson for $35. She later received a diamond ring and Nike stock.

TIFF (Tagged Image File Format): One of several formats for compressing graphic images to make smaller digital files. The images in this book are TIFFs. Websites generally use JPGs or GIFs. TIFF file names end in .tif.

Thin space: Narrower than a regular space. Used between the dots in an **ellipsis**: …, not ... (very subtle difference) or . . .

Title: In addition to the name of a book, it's book-biz jargon for a specific variety of book—but not an individual physical book. "Wow! Did you hear that PassKey Publications is putting out 50 titles this year? That's nearly twice as many as last year."

Title page: The recto (right-hand) page at the beginning of a book that shows the book's title, subtitle, author's name, publisher and perhaps other information.

TK: Shorthand for "To Come," a notation made on a layout to show that an element (such as a photograph or chart) will be provided later and space should be reserved for it.

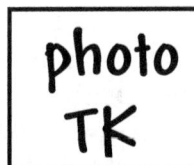

Tracking: Adjusting the spaces between letters in one or more words. Tracking and **kerning** are types of **letter spacing**, but letter spacing usually means tracking.

Trade paperback: A book like the one you are reading now, with a cardboard cover, bigger pages and better grade of paper than used for mass-market paperbacks.

Trade publishing: Traditional book publishing where a publisher pays an advance and perhaps royalties on books sold.

Trim size: The final width and height of a book page and covers after the book is bound and trimmed. This book is trimmed to be six by nine inches—a common size.

True Type: A type font standard, originally developed by Apple in the 1980s to compete with Adobe's PostScript fonts. Microsoft soon added TrueType fonts to Windows, most notably the ubiquitous **Times New Roman** and **Arial**.

Typeface: A distinct family of type, such as Andy, **Rockwell, ALGERIAN, Verdana, Elephant** or **Franklin Gothic.**

Typesetting: Formatting a document on a computer to produce page layouts suitable for printing. In the past, actual pieces of type were arranged to form words and pages.

Typo: Short for **typographical error**, an error on a typed or printed page, sign, web page, etc. caused by equipment or finger failure—not by lack of knowledge.

Underrun: Book printing that results in fewer books than ordered due to damage (*spoilage*) during printing. An underrun of up to 10% is considered acceptable.

University press: A publishing business owned by a college or university. Most of its books are written by professors who teach or do research at the institution.

Unsolicited manuscript: A manuscript sent to a publisher that did not request it in advance. Most large publishers do not accept unsolicited manuscripts.

URL (Uniform Resource Locator): A web address.

Vanity press (vanity publisher): A publisher paid by authors to publish their books. The term has negative connotations.

Virgule: A forward slash (/). It's also the French word for "comma." (Merci beaucoup, Mademoiselle Sheila.)

Virtual Book Tour (VBT): An online simulation of a physical book tour, where an author would travel to be interviewed and sign books. In a virtual version, an author "visits" websites and blogs to be interviewed and to answer questions, and may write something special or post a book excerpt.

Wholesaler: A "middleman" company which buys books from a publisher and sells them to a retailer. Unlike a distributor, a wholesaler usually just fills orders and does not have an active sales force.

Sum werdz too wotch owte four

Accommodate has a double "c" AND a double "m."

A lot is two words, not one.

Argument does not have an "e" like "argue."

Awhile or **A while** can both be legitimate. The noun is spelled as two words: "I napped for a while." The adverb is spelled as a single word: "I napped awhile."

Believe follows the old "i-before-e except after c" rule. However, **foreign, forfeit, sovereign, surfeit, caffeine, casein, codeine, either, geisha, inveigle, keister, leisure, neither, protein, seize, sheik,** and **Sheila** do not.

Bellwether has nothing to do with the weather. A "wether" is a castrated sheep or goat that wears a bell and leads a herd. The lack of cojones made it less likely that the leader of the pack would stray.

Cannot v. can not: "Cannot" is one word. It is **never** split into two words. If you want to stress the "not" part of the word, either CAPITALIZE the entire word; put the entire word in **boldface** or *italics*; or, if your word processor permits you to do so, put the "not" segment of the word in boldface (can**not**) or italics (can*not*), or use an underscore (can-*not*).

Carburetor has just one "a," like "car."

  Cemetery does not end in "ary" or begin with "s."

Changeable, unlike **argument**, retains its "e" so you know the "g" is soft, pronounced like "j."

  Collectible is not "able." No rule applies here, just memory.

Coolly has a double "l" when it's not a noun. When it is a noun, it's spelled "coolie."

Criteria v. criterion: Confusing these two nouns is a common error, even among highly educated people. "Criteria" is the plural of "criterion," but many people aren't even aware of the word "criterion." If you're discussing various requirements that must be met, use "criteria" but if you are writing about one major requirement to be met, use "criterion." (During Sheila's many years as a technical writer, one of her colleagues — an English major who graduated from a top college — was working on a software users' manual that dealt with various criteria. But, when this writer referred to one criterion, she continued to use "criteria." How did she graduate, especially as an English major?)

Deceive does obey the "i before e except after c" rule. So does **receive**, but not **frequencies** or **science** or **species**.

Drunkenness should have a double "n" when spelled by sober people.

   Dumbbell has a double "b," you **dummy** (not "dumby").

   Embarrass (ment) has a double "r" and a double "s."

Epic is a big important book, poem, or movie. **Epoch** is an important era. You can write an epic about an epoch.

Exceed does not end with "cede." Nothing exceeds like excess.

Existence does not have an "a."

Flier is someone who flies (not "flys"). It's also a leaflet, or a golf ball that goes too far. Airlines frequently say "frequent flyer." They're frequently wrong.

Flyer can be part of a proper name for transportation ("Radio Flyer," "Flexible Flyer," "Rocky Mountain Flyer") or a sports team ("Philadelphia Flyers" and "Dayton Flyers"), or even sneakers ("PF Flyers").

Gauge is a verb or a noun with a silent "u." For the thickness of wire or metal, or the space between train rails, or the size of a shotgun, you can ditch the "u." **Gouge** means to scoop, dig, swindle, or extort; or a tool for gouging.

Grateful has just one "e." It's not so great. It has the same root as "gratitude."

Guarantee does not end like "warranty" except in a proper name like Morgan Guaranty Trust.

Harass has just one set of double letters.

Inoculate has no double letters.

Jibe (NOT **Jive**) means to agree. Jibe and **gibe** mean to taunt. Jibe also means to move a sail to change direction.

Layout is a noun. **Lay out** is a verb. A designer will lay out a layout.

Lightning is the spark in the sky, or part of the name of Lightning Source, the printer of many POD books. **Lightening** removes weight.

Maintenance has just one "ain," unlike "**maintain**."

Maneuver is a French-ish word, that's easier to spell than the British version: "**manoeuvre**."

Medieval refers to the MIDdle Ages, but is spelled more like "**medium**." Some of those wacky Brits use "**mediaeval**."

Memento reminds you of a moment, but the first vowel is an "e" not an "o." Don't ask why; just remember it.

Millennium was spelled wrong millions of times back in 1999 and 2000. It still is. It gets a double "l" and a double "n."

Minuscule means mini, but it's spelled more like "minus" (except when it's being spelled by people who prefer "**miniscule**.") Pick one version, and be consistent.

Misspell is frequently misspelled. It needs a double "s" but no hyphen.

Noticeable gets a silent "e" to keep the "c" from being pronounced like a "k."

Occasionally has a double set of double consonants

Occurrence has two traps: the occurrence of *double* double consonants, and "ence" not "ance" at the end.

Pharaoh uses the "a" twice.

Plenitude is right. **Plentitude** is wrong, but is used a lot.

Possession possesses two double letters.

Principal is a school's boss or the most important element of something. A **principle** is a rule or an important point.

Privilege is not edgy. It has no "d."

Reevaluate does not have a hyphen.

Relevant is not "revelant," "revelent" or "relevent."

Separate has an "a" as the second vowel.

Sergeant, unlike the affectionate "Sarge," has no "a" up front, but it does have a silent "a" later on.

Sleight of hand is a group of techniques magicians use to secretly manipulate objects. It's not "slight of hand" or "slide of hand, "Sleight" comes from an Old Norse word for cleverness, cunning, and slyness

Supersede is not spelled like "succeed" or "precede" and may be the only "sede" word we have.

Threshold does not have a double "h."

Until gets just one "l" even though it's often a perfect substitute for "till." Wilson Pickett sang, *Wait Till the Midnight Hour* or *Wait 'Til the Midnight Hour*, depending on who transcribed the lyrics.

Weird is weird because it breaks the "i before e except after c." rule. **Seize** is weird, too.

Michael N. Marcus has been a journalist, author, publisher, advertising copywriter, publicist, photographer, band manager, amateur attorney, golf ball diver, recording engineer, and is founder and president of Able-Comm, Inc. ("The Telecom Department Store").

His writing career started when he published a newspaper in elementary school, and since then he has been an editor at *Rolling Stone* and has written for many other magazines and newspapers. Michael has provided the words for over one hundred websites and blogs. He specializes in making technology understandable, and often humorous.

Born in New York in 1946, Michael's a proud member of the first cohort of the Baby Boom.

At the urging of a misguided guidance counselor, he went to Lehigh University to become an electrical engineer and was quickly disappointed to learn that engineering was mostly math—and slide rules were not nearly as much fun as soldering irons.

Michael was one of the few literate people in his engineer-filled freshman dormitory and made money by editing term papers for classmates. He got into big trouble when he was caught running wire from his dorm room to a friend's room two floors below, and when an inspector found a payphone in his suitcase.

Later, his college apartment had an elaborate and illegal multi-line phone system, a phone booth with a toilet in it, and an invisible phone activated by two handclaps.

Michael lives in Connecticut with his wife Marilyn, Hunter the Golden Retriever, and a lot of stuff—including both indoor and outdoor telephone booths, a "Lily Tomlin" switchboard, lots of books, CDs and DVDs, and many black boxes with flashing lights. Marilyn is very tolerant.

More about Michael: www.MichaelMarc.us

Photo and illustration credits

Images listed below are believed to be "public domain."
◆Groucho Marx photo from the *New York World-Telegram and the Sun* Newspaper Photograph Collection, Library of Congress ◆Dorothy Parker photo from Bain News Service via Library of Congress ◆Voltaire painting by Nicolas de Largillière ◆G. K. Chesterton photo from The American Chesterton Society ◆Roget illustration from Thomas Pettigrew

Photos of Young, Sampson and Spears were provided for publicity purposes.

Photo of car in front of house by Jason Stitt, via Fotolia.com

Floppy disk photo from Maxell

Syringe photo from llandrea

Radio Flyer photo from Radio Flyer

Back cover photo of author by Victoria Scopetta

NOTE: Some books shown on the following pages may not be available yet. Some cover designs may change.

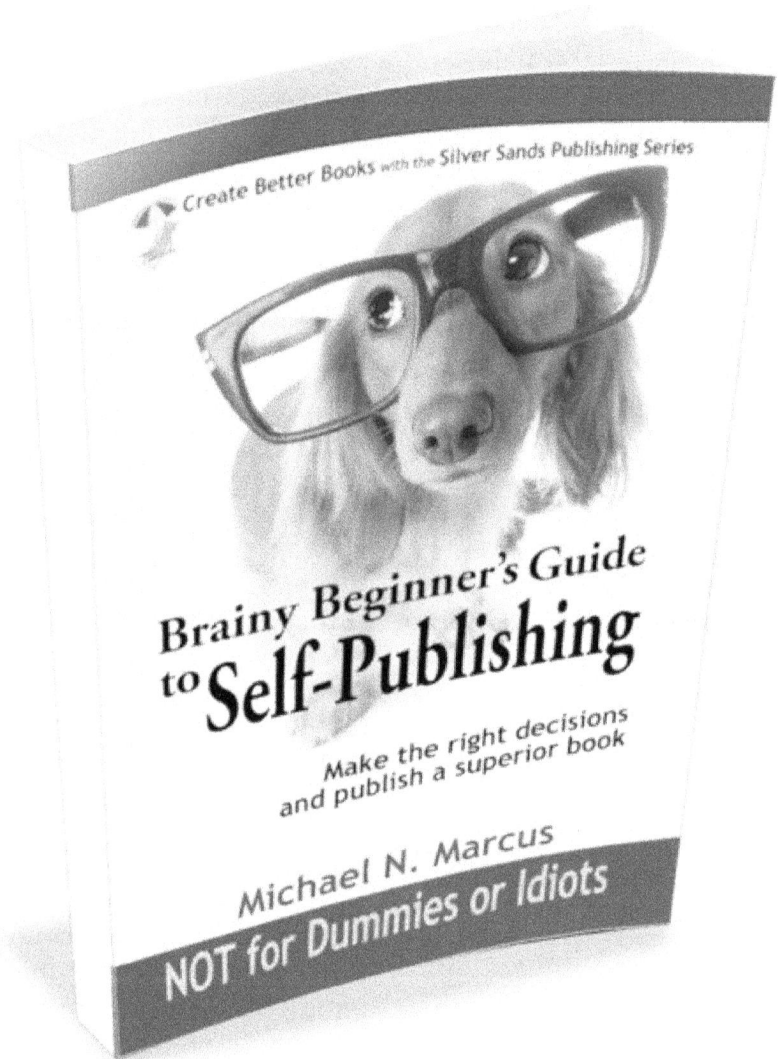

Create Better Books *with the* Silver Sands Publishing Series

Brainy Beginner's Guide
to Self-Publishing

Make the right decisions
and publish a superior book

Michael N. Marcus

NOT for Dummies or Idiots

There are books about self-publishing for "dummies" and "complete idiots." Dummies and idiots can't publish books, and probably shouldn't write them. This book is for smart writers—but not necessarily geniuses—who want to learn about self-publishing. It's also for people who like funny pictures of dogs wearing oversize eyeglasses. At Amazon, Barnes & Noble and other booksellers.

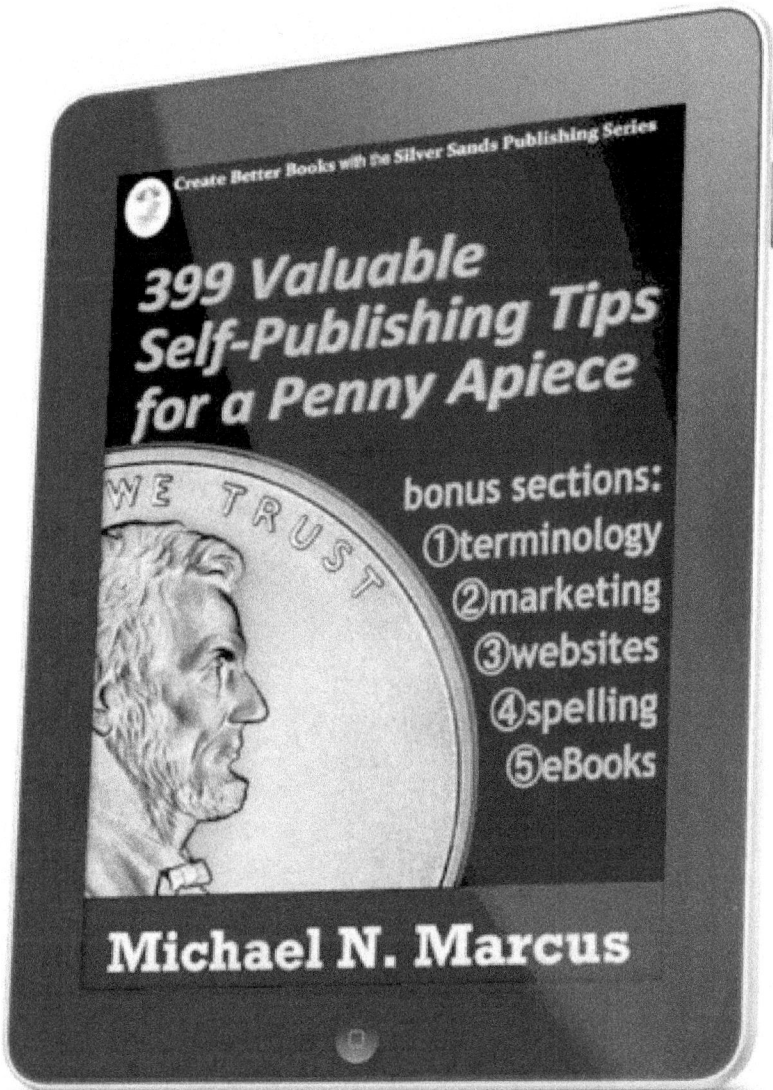

Create Better Books with the Silver Sands Publishing Series

399 Valuable
Self-Publishing Tips
for a Penny Apiece

IN WE TRUST

bonus sections:
①terminology
②marketing
③websites
④spelling
⑤eBooks

Michael N. Marcus

Available as an e-book only—in multiple formats—this is a collection of important advice worth *much* more than $3.99

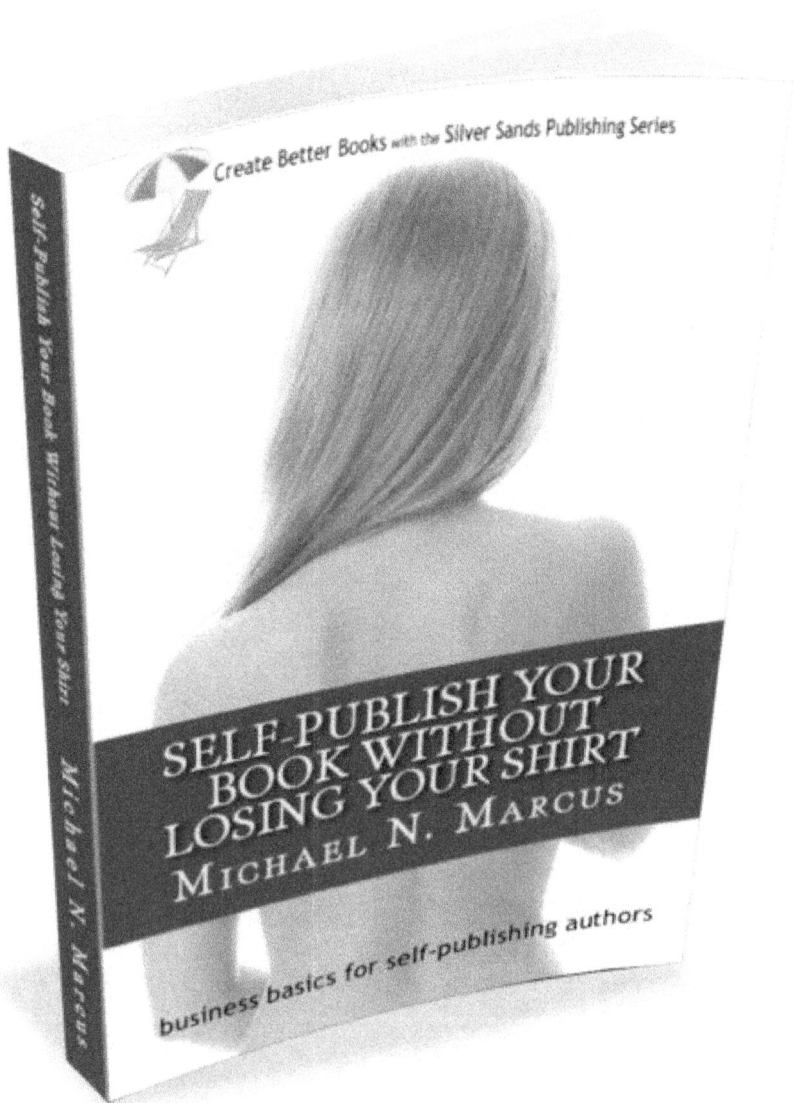

If you are an author who spends money for publishing and promotion, you are not just an artist. You are running a business. This book will help you do it the right way. At Amazon, Barnes & Noble and other booksellers.

Create Better Books *with the* Silver Sands Publishing Series

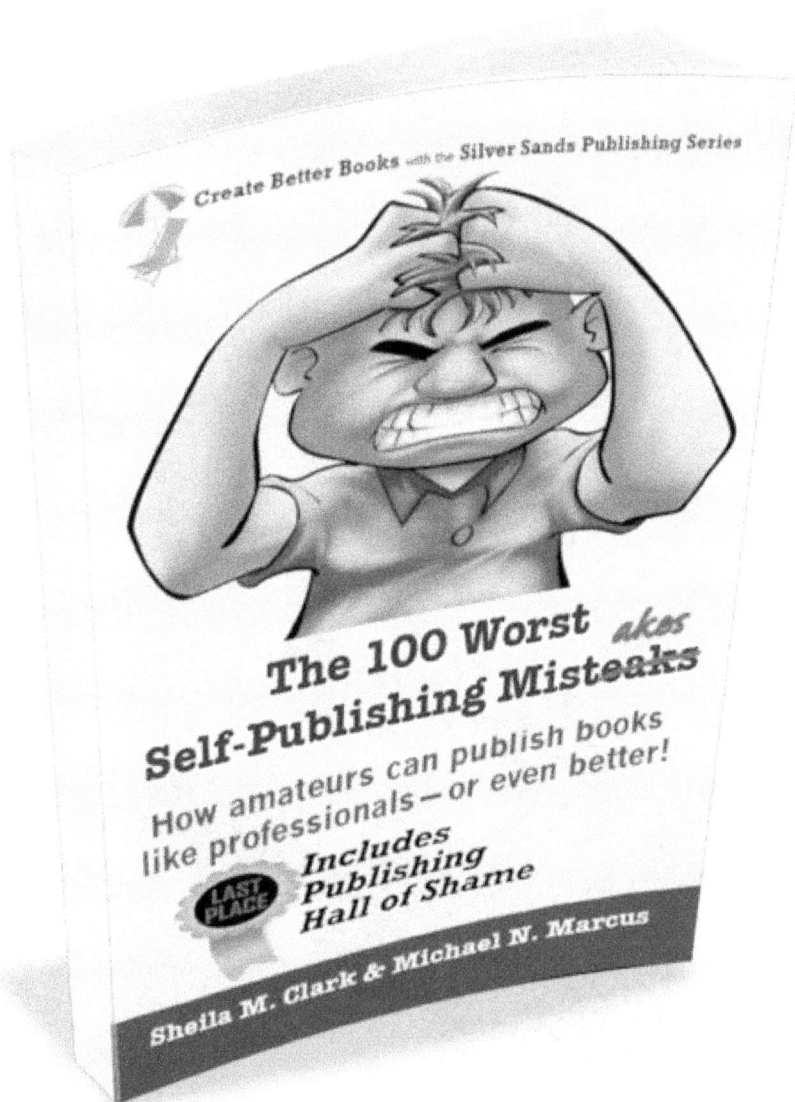

The 100 Worst *akes*
Self-Publishing Misteaks

How amateurs can publish books
like professionals—or even better!

LAST PLACE

Includes
Publishing
Hall of Shame

Sheila M. Clark & Michael N. Marcus

An expansion of the book you are now reading, with advice on avoiding over 100 terrible mistakes in all areas of self-publishing. At Amazon, Barnes & Noble and other booksellers.

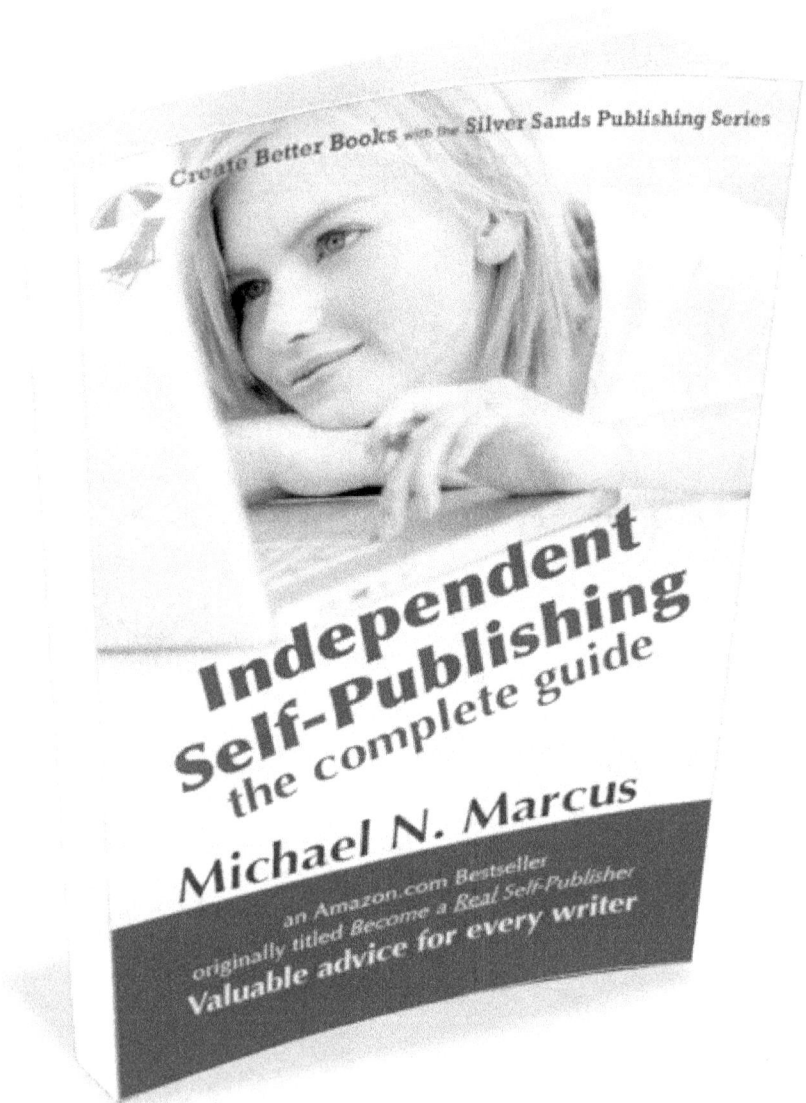

An update of an Amazon bestseller, this book is for the writer who wants to be the boss and maybe make more money than if she or he used a self-publishing company. At Amazon, Barnes & Noble and other booksellers.

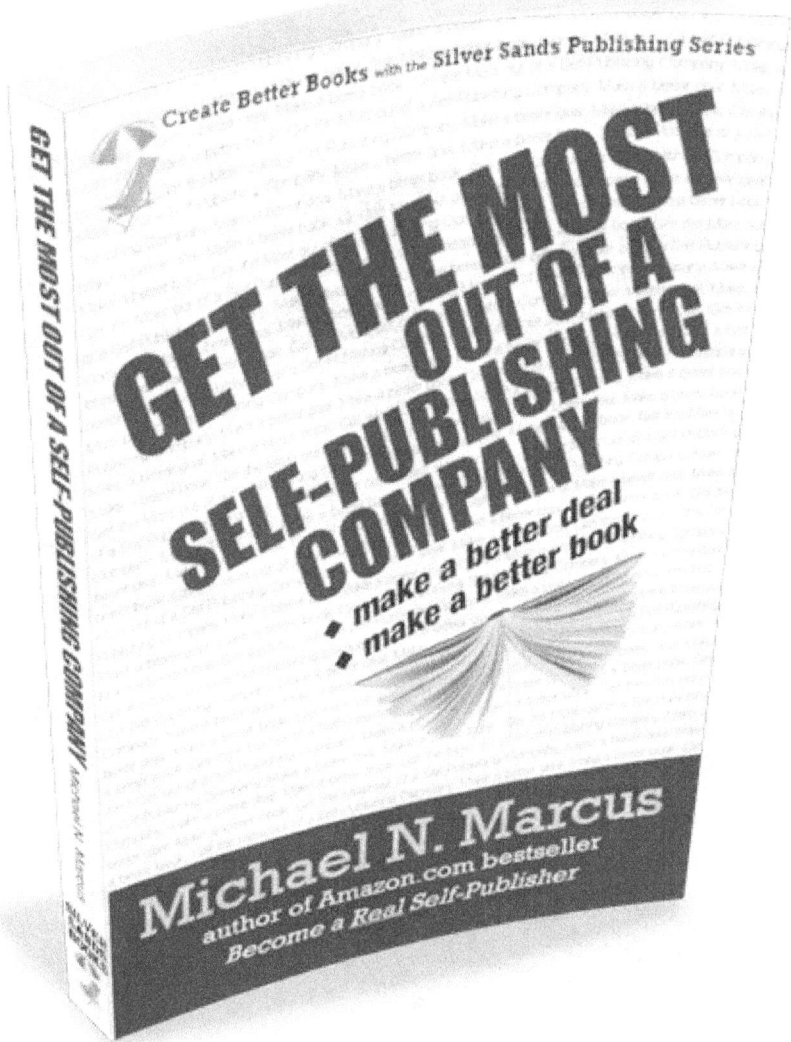

The authoritative book for authors who use self-publishing companies. At Amazon, Barnes & Noble and other booksellers.

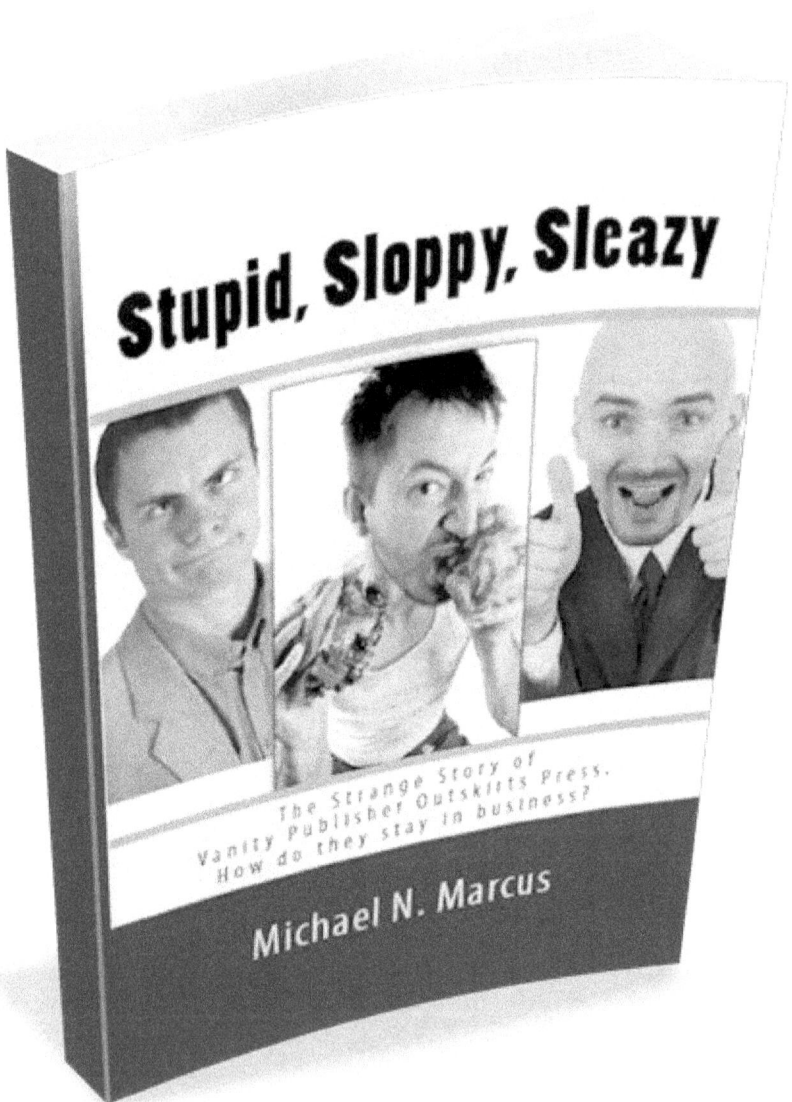

Stupid, Sloppy, Sleazy

The Strange Story of Vanity Publisher Outskirts Press. How do they stay in business?

Michael N. Marcus

For any writer considering publishing through Outskirts Press. Revealing, infuriating... and funny. At Amazon, Barnes & Noble and other booksellers.

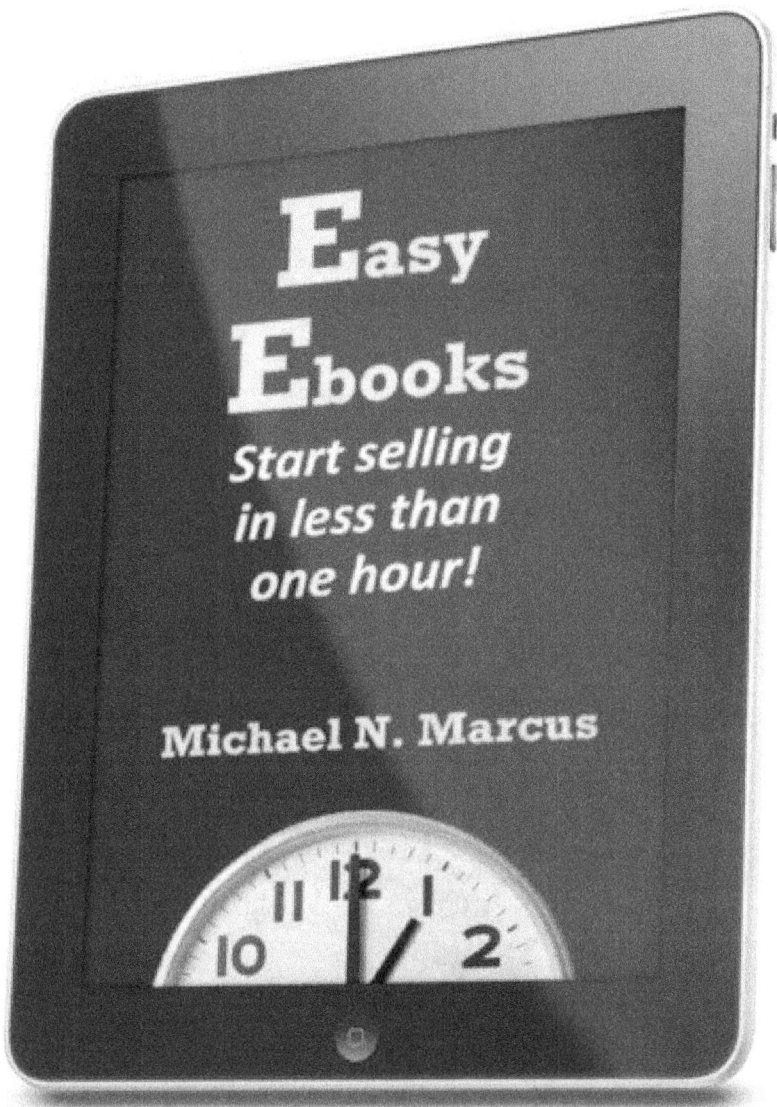

Easy
Ebooks
*Start selling
in less than
one hour!*

Michael N. Marcus

This book, published both electronically and on paper, will show you how to produce and promote a high-quality e-book. You can start selling e-books in less than one hour after a p-book is completed.

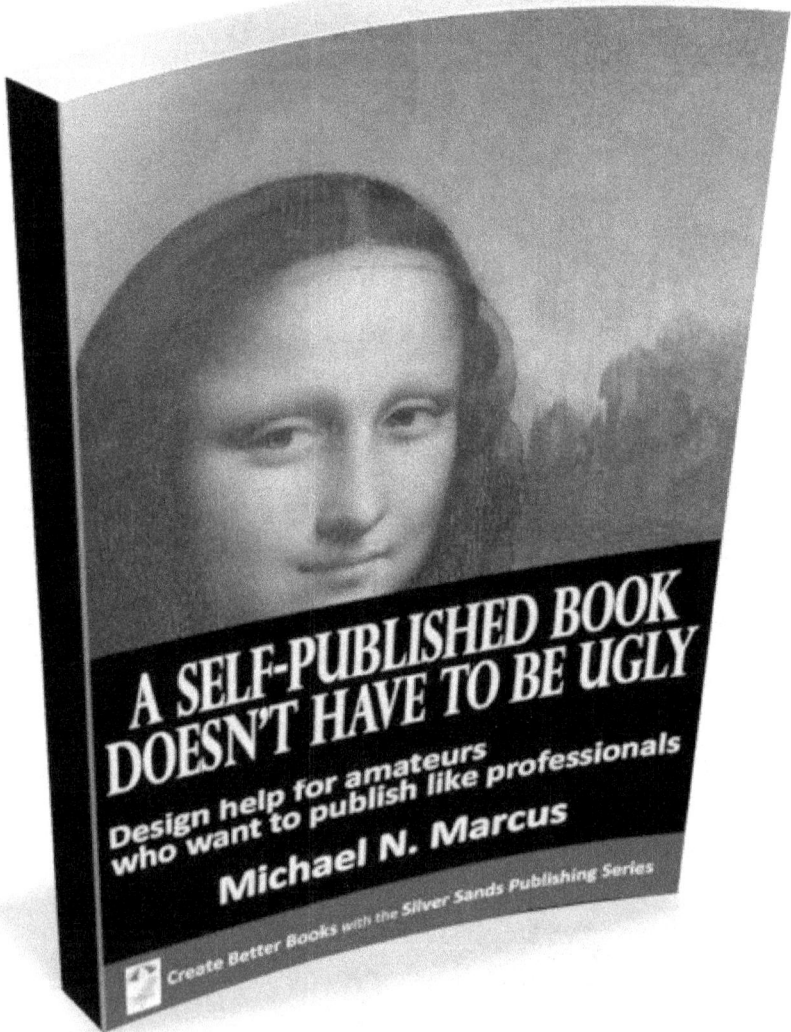

A SELF-PUBLISHED BOOK DOESN'T HAVE TO BE UGLY

Design help for amateurs who want to publish like professionals

Michael N. Marcus

Create Better Books with the Silver Sands Publishing Series

Most self-published books look much worse than books from the major publishers. It doesn't have to be that way. This book will help you to avoid making awful mistakes. At Amazon, Barnes & Noble and other booksellers.

Create Better Books with the Silver Sands Publishing Series

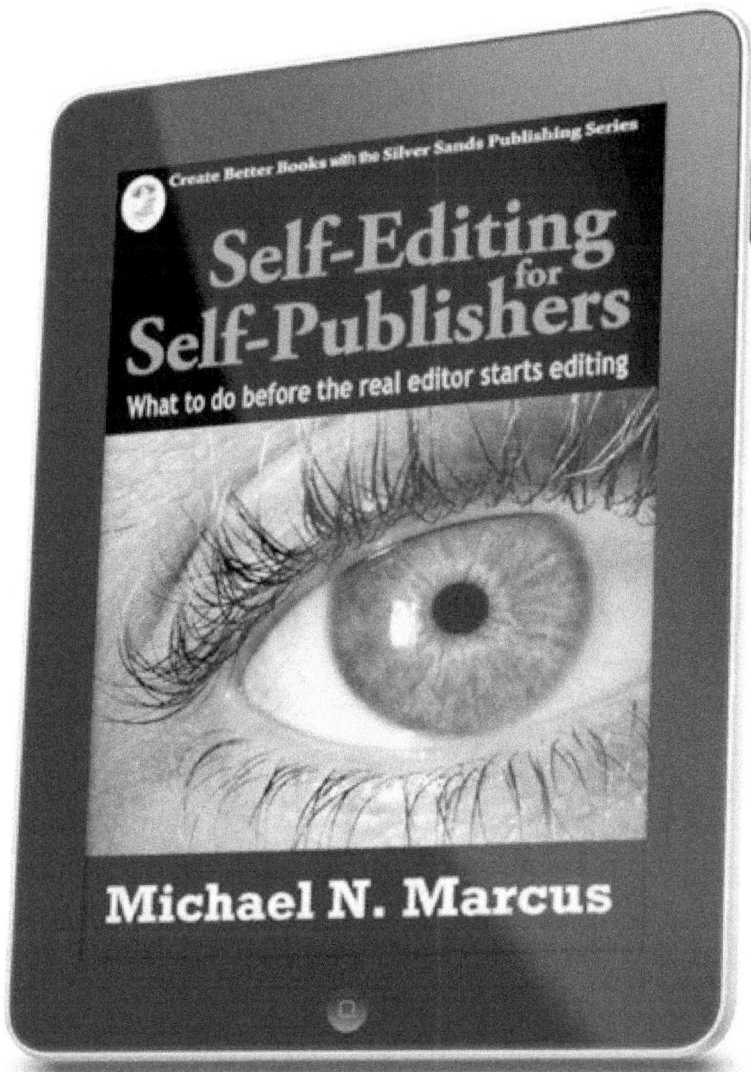

Self-Editing for Self-Publishers

What to do before the real editor starts editing

Michael N. Marcus

No writer should be her only editor, but she has to be *one* of the editors. The more you self-edit, before the pro gets started, the better the book will be. You might even save money. Multiple e-book formats.

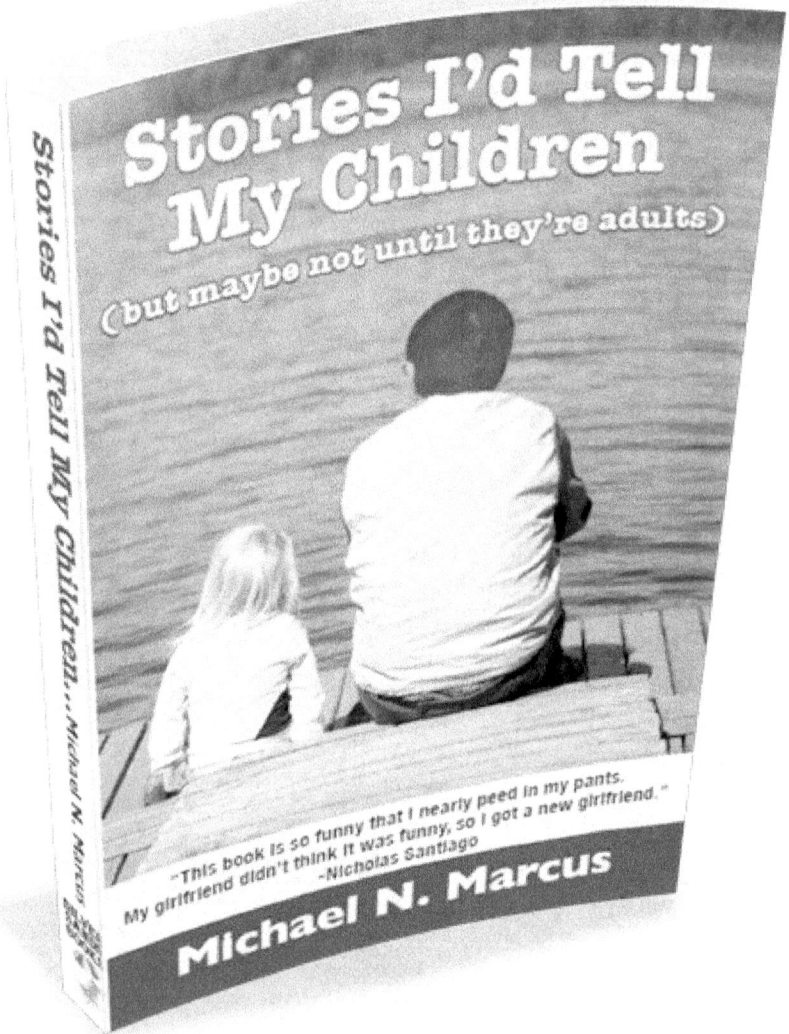

Extremely funny, often raunchy, and sometimes poignant. Guaranteed to be at least 80% true. At Amazon, Barnes & Noble and other booksellers as a paperback, hardcover, and in multiple e-book formats.

Printed in the USA
CPSIA information can be obtained
at www.ICGtesting.com
LVHW021213051123
762922LV00036B/247

9 780983 057253